THE ART OF
Emily Dickinson's
EARLY POETRY

THE ART OF

Emily Dickinson's

EARLY POETRY

BY

DAVID T. PORTER

HARVARD UNIVERSITY PRESS

Cambridge, Massachusetts

1 9 6 6

Distributed in Great Britain by Oxford University Press, London

Poems by Emily Dickinson included in this volume are reprinted by permission of the President and Fellows of Harvard College and the Trustees of Amherst College from THE
POEMS OF EMILY DICKINSON, edited by Thomas H.
Johnson, The Belknap Press of Harvard University Press,
Cambridge, Mass., copyright, 1951 and 1955, by the President
and Fellows of Harvard College.

Publication of this book has been aided by a grant from the
Ford Foundation

Library of Congress Catalog Card Number 66-13182

Printed in the United States of America

*To Bertha Thomas Porter
and to the memory of
Roy Avery Porter*

CONTENTS

PREFACE

Two facts urged the undertaking of this study. The first is that Emily Dickinson's singularity as a poet resides not in what she believes — for her interests and her convictions are not original — but rather in the way she speaks to us: her voice is unique. The important critical works, however, are more concerned with her themes than with her artistic techniques. The second fact is that the developmental course of her poetic career remains uncharted. Richard B. Sewall reminds us that "there are still mysteries — for instance, the different phases of her career cannot be neatly articulated." Richard Chase suggested a first approach more than twenty years ago, when he concluded that "the story of her poetic development between the ages of twenty and thirty-two [1850–1862], if it could be told with any exactitude, would be concerned . . . with her technical and stylistic development and generally advancing maturity rather than with the discovery of her basic themes. For these she already had as early as 1850." My inquiry has the specific purpose of plotting the boundary of the developmental period in her career and discovering the early stylistic habits that equipped her for the enormous flood of poetry in the year 1862 and after. Its more general purpose is to formulate the attitudes of mind and art by which we identify this remarkable poet. The paradox, if we must find one, is that we discern such formal brilliance in a body of poetry that everywhere seizes our imagination by its surface currents of rushing spontaneity.

Recognition of Emily Dickinson's strength of command over her nervous expression in the early years not only makes more credible the seemingly headlong composition of the three hundred sixty-six poems assigned to the single year 1862 by Thomas

H. Johnson, but also demands our awareness that she composed with purpose and conviction. We should be careful not to dismiss all of her unconventional stylistic mannerisms as idiosyncratic and gratuitous or condescend to the myth of the spontaneously creative private poet. Moreover, an understanding of the ideas and style persistent in the early poetry will help us to a perspective from which a further search for developmental patterns may be launched.

I believe that to every artist a conventional vocabulary of basic forms is indispensable as a starting point for the creative gesture, and I have therefore organized the central chapters of this book with regard to the fundamental matters of metrics and rhyme, imagery and diction, speaker and language usage. These are the schema Emily Dickinson necessarily employed. We come to know her better as we see how she travels what Ernst Gombrich calls the long road through schema and correction. I have tried to show how these various technical elements cohere within the theme that obsessed her. I have quoted a great deal from her work, but there seems no other satisfactory way of validating my conclusions. My intent, nevertheless, is to exemplify rather than to exhaust by tedious demonstration. Even so, some repetitious use of particular poems is unavoidable, since certain works are useful in demonstrating more than one element under discussion. In a few instances, I have turned to later poems when I believed they would help define particular habits in the early work.

Other critical problems remain and are even more formidable. Emily Dickinson wrote over seventeen hundred poems, all of them brief. Lacking any composition of prolonged development, the critic is unable to press his own convictions by a sustained look at a single work. To attempt to encompass this large, fragmented canon, or even a part of it as I have, involves the danger that the final product will have only a specious unity, a sort of grotesque resurrection. Generalizations about her work must be made in the knowledge that exceptions are rife, though perhaps not always significantly contradictory. With his privileged perspective, the critic assumes the obligation to be tactful and not to make the poetry seem more coherent or sound better than it is. The same caveat applies to schematizing the poet's development. We prefer absolutes, and perhaps we would like to see Emily Dickinson's emotional progression as the working out, for example, of "The slow exchange of Hope–/ For something passiver–," as she says in one of her poems, but we know better. Her moods vary, her techniques revert to the facile compromise. There are early poems of profound resignation, just as there are late poems of excruciating hopefulness.

Underlying all the questions whose answers we seek is the problem of chronology. Emily Dickinson's apparent habit of making undated fair copies of her poems and then destroying her worksheets prevents the establishment of exact dates of composition or even of fair copies. For the majority of the manuscripts, Johnson determines dates by the character of the handwriting. In almost all cases he is able only to date them by years rather than by month or week. Within each particular year, he has arranged the poems according to their relative state of completion, i.e., the first poems are fair copies to recipients, followed by fair copies which were uncirculated. These are followed by poems in semifinal draft (in the order in which the poet placed them in her packets) and by poems in worksheet stage. Because the dating is approximate I have used, besides the sixteen poems she enclosed in letters to Thomas Wentworth Higginson in 1862 (the year and the correspondence which, I believe, mark the end of the formative period), only the 301 poems dated 1861 and earlier (numbers 67, 86, and 216 appear in both groups). It is impossible to determine poems she may have written between the end of 1861 and the first letter to Higginson on April 15, 1862.

The poems dated through 1861 are numbers 1 through 298,

plus numbers 330, 331, and 687. The poems enclosed in the 1862 letters to Higginson are numbers 67, 86, 216, 299, 318–328, and 365. The value of these earlier poems as evidence of artistic habits in that particular chronological period is enhanced by the certainty that these works were indeed composed early. The fair copies, that is, establish a clear *terminus ad quem*. One cannot be certain, on the other hand, how many of the later poems, dated through the years to 1886, were in fact composed long before she made fair copies of them.

I have avoided biographical interpretations of the poems, not because that approach is wholly fruitless, but because it is excessively speculative. We need not be troubled by wonder or frustration at the refusal of the *life* to explain the *poetry*. If anyone requires a demonstration that an artist can create situations he has not experienced, let him read *The Red Badge of Courage* in the knowledge that Crane had never gone to war. We need not commit the fallacy of believing Emily Dickinson *felt* sad when she wrote of sadness, nor need we succumb to the fetish of the single cause by trying to locate exact springs of creativity. We cannot make art mean to us what it meant to its creator. That way, Gombrich reminds us, is barred by the angel with the flaming sword.

Whatever forms of anxiety Emily Dickinson actually experienced, we know her condition released great art, and that after all is what is important now. We know what the poetry discloses. Her life and her poetry were a constant assaying and rejection of cant. The conflict was very private and she was an intensely personal poet: her world acquired its meaning in the way it ravaged the individual. This is why her work has an irrepressible personality and presence about it. Her success is that while she was intensely personal and particular, she was able to convey general truths of the human condition. By her poetry she apprehended the world and, perhaps as much for her as for us, that poetry helps us to confront life's profoundest necessities.

With all other recent investigators of the work of Emily Dickinson, I am deeply indebted to Thomas H. Johnson, whose editions of the poems and letters make available the complete texts indispensable to a critical study of the poet. I have transcribed Emily Dickinson's work as it appears in the Johnson editions, including her spelling errors and vagaries of punctuation. Where necessary, however, I have substituted a period at the end of the last line of quoted portions in place of the poet's characteristic dash. The index of first lines of the early poems provides complete cross references to both the discussions of specific works and their texts included in this study.

For his abundant and rigorous counsel and for his friendship, I am especially grateful to an exemplary scholar, William H. Gilman. For their posing of the hard questions that made me reconsider many of my judgments, I thank Howard C. Horsford and Richard B. Sewall. Encouragement in times of indecision came pointedly from R. James Kaufmann, Sidney Kaplan, Howard O. Brogan and Mark Carroll. I trust I have adequately acknowledged in end notes the Dickinson scholars whose commentary helped develop or affirm my own convictions. M. Kathleen Ahern has been a perceptive and meticulous editor. If there are lapses in critical tact, however, they are mine alone.

The staffs of the libraries of the University of Rochester, the University of Massachusetts, and Amherst College, and of the Jones Library, Amherst, and the Houghton Library have been helpful, as always. For timely assistance I am also indebted to Dean Allen and Dorothy Miles Pixley. Joan Weston expertly typed and retyped the manuscripts.

My sons, Tom and Dave, had a refreshingly small tolerance for authorial solemnity. I hope that virtue is reflected here. My wife, Lee, in countless ways, made the book possible.

Research grants from the University of Rochester and the University of Massachusetts contributed to the preparation of this study. Quotations from Emily Dickinson's work are reprinted by permission of the publishers and the Trustees of Amherst College from Thomas H. Johnson, editor, *The Poems of Emily Dickinson* and Thomas H. Johnson and Theodora V. W. Ward, editors, *The Letters of Emily Dickinson,* Cambridge, Mass.: The Belknap Press of Harvard University Press, Copyright 1955, 1958, and by the President and Fellows of Harvard College. By permission of Little, Brown and Co., from Thomas H. Johnson, editor, *The Complete Poems of Emily Dickinson,* the following poems are reprinted in whole or in part: numbers 7, 10, 11, 14, 61, 63, 81, 153, Copyright 1914, 1942 by Martha Dickinson Bianchi; numbers 173, 243, 257, 282, 285, 293, 326, 341, 479, 652, 657, 673, 745, Copyright 1929, 1957 by Mary L. Hampson; numbers 144, 169, 204, 236, 240, 263, 264, 281, 283, 286, 292, 295, 408, 451, 963, Copyright 1935 by Martha Dickinson Bianchi; number 9, Copyright 1924 by Martha Dickinson Bianchi. Passages from numbers 5, 15, 104, 159, and 298 are reprinted from Martha D. Bianchi, *The Life and Letters of Emily Dickinson* and *Emily Dickinson Face to Face* by permission of Houghton Mifflin Company. Grateful acknowledgement is made to Holt, Rinehart and Winston for permission to quote from Charles Anderson, *Emily Dickinson's Poetry: Stairway of Surprise,* to Penguin Books for a passage from Philip Wayne's translation of *Faust,* and to Harvard University Press for quotations from Henry W. Foote, *Three Centuries of American Hymnody.*

An earlier version of Chapter One, "Emily Dickinson: The Formative Years," appeared in *The Massachusetts Review.*

Nantucket   D. T. P.
July 9, 1965

THE ART OF
Emily Dickinson's
EARLY POETRY

Now the zest of romanticism consists in taking what you know is an independent and ancient world as if it were material for your private emotions.

GEORGE SANTAYANA

→» I «←

THE FORMATIVE YEARS

I know the Art
I mention–easy–Here–

It's full as Opera.

Emily Dickinson, 1862 [1]

Emily Dickinson contrived her encounters with the world, for though her creative life was adventurous, its vital nerve lodged precariously open to the aroused emotions. One of her protective strategies was to dispatch her voice to divert the clumsy world from that obsessively guarded precinct. Her several public selves inhabit the letters. The voice she sent to Thomas Wentworth Higginson, her critic in the literary world, argued her awkwardness and sought instruction. "Could you tell me how to grow?" she asked.[2] But we misjudge her attitude to her poetic ability and never reach the heart of her creative force unless we search beyond the diffident surrogate posing in the letters. For by 1862, even as she begged Higginson to be her tutor, Emily Dickinson was confident her frugal lines had attained artistic relevance. This knowledge may anchor for us the shifting critical speculations about the season when, in Milton's term, she recognized the inward ripeness.

Sharp differences of opinion exist concerning the direction of Emily Dickinson's development as an artist. Charles R. Anderson asserts "there are no marked periods in her career, no significant curve of development in her artistic powers, no progressive con-

cern with different genres."[3] Austin Warren has declared that
the theory of her systematic growth from writing conventional
and sentimental pieces to a mature and individual manner is
"too neat." He adds: "Emily did, to the end, 'look back.' Unlike
Mozart and Beethoven and Hopkins and James, she had no
'late manner' so integrally held that she could not, in conscience,
deviate therefrom."[4] Nicholas Joost declares that Emily Dickinson "apparently has been the one example in the world's history
of a great poet whose poetry shows no development in ideas and
technique."[5]

Though he did not have the benefit of a comprehensive dating
of the fair copies, G. F. Whicher said of Emily Dickinson's love
poems that they are "successive moments in the intricate progress
of a soul through the deepest of human experiences."[6] The
mode of succession Whicher deduces appears to be an imposed
pattern which orders the poetic statements according to whether
they represent the anguish of an early and impossible love or a
stoic accommodation later to separation from a lover. The patterning reflects a conventional notion of the progress of love,
and skirts the vexing suspicion that some of the works were
composed in periods of reflection long after the germinal experience or, indeed, in conjecture and imaginative projection distinct from actual experience. Theodora Ward, similarly, looks
to seeming facts of the poet's life to find an ordering pattern for
the works: "Out of this dark period [of 1857] she emerged with
more definiteness in the year 1858, when the assembling of the
first packets of poems marked the beginning of the real flowering
of her creative genius."[7] Like Whicher, in her assessment of the
general tendency of Emily Dickinson's poetic expression, Mrs.
Ward works from the assumption that the poems somehow
chronicle the poet's struggle to overcome a personal problem:
"She consciously took the artist's path to peace, and worked her
way through deep and agonizing conflict, recording the steps in
her poems."[8] Thomas H. Johnson, however, believes the first

poems Emily Dickinson sent to Higginson indicate the culmination of a developmental period. The four poems she initially selected for Higginson, he says, "reveal that in 1862 the poet was no longer a novice but an artist whose strikingly original talent was fully developed."[9] This view is somewhat altered from that in his introduction to *The Letters of Emily Dickinson*, in which he asserts that "Emily Dickinson's full maturity as a dedicated artist occurred during the span of the Civil War."[10] Elsewhere Mr. Johnson acknowledges the poet's awareness of her talent significantly earlier. In an essay published while the variorum edition was still in preparation, he declared: "All who have had access to material touching upon Emily Dickinson's life and writing agree — I think without exception — that she knew during her twenties [1850 to 1860] that she was uncommonly gifted."[11] Again, in the introduction to *Letters*, he suggests that the time of her serious application to the art of poetry occurred as early as 1850. He writes: "The fantastic letters in the early part of 1850 lead to the speculation that this might have been the period when she commenced in earnest to write poetry."[12] Northrup Frye, commenting recently on Emily Dickinson's artistic development, declares that "she seems, after her early valentines [1850–1852], to have reached her mature style almost in a single bound."[13]

The single event which first revealed the strength of Emily Dickinson's engagement in her art was the appearance of Higginson's "Letter to a Young Contributor" in the *Atlantic Monthly* for April 1862. It is a curious essay, a clutter of both trivial and incisive advice to writers. The tone alters from genuine interest in the furtherance of art to elegant condescension, pomposity, and commonplace moralizing. It digresses on the comparable values of literary and military fame (Higginson took command of a Union Army regiment in November of the same year), and closes with the banal assertion that to the artist, once dead and securely situated in heaven, earthly fortunes and fame are of no

consequence. There is even advice on the conduct of the worth-
while life: "War or peace, fame or forgetfulness, can bring no
real injury to one who has formed the fixed purpose to live
nobly day by day." [14]

Yet "Letter to a Young Contributor" drew an immediate
response from the poet. The world had indeed written to her,
and in a most disarming way: "So large a proportion of 'Atlantic' readers," Higginson announced, "either might, would, could,
or should be 'Atlantic' contributors . . . that this epistle will be
sure of perusal." [15] The invitation offered a confrontation of poet
and editor, remote, impersonal, the kind Emily Dickinson could
safely conduct across the protective distance traversed only by the
postal service. On his part, Higginson was distressingly patronizing. "To take the lead in bringing forward a new genius," he
declares, is a "fascinating privilege." The satisfaction, he says, is
comparable to "that of the physician who boasted to Sir Henry
Halford of having been the first man to discover the Asiatic
cholera and to communicate it to the public." [16] The analogy
embarrasses us, but it did not deter Emily Dickinson. An attentive and resigned watcher of the world's vanities, she dominated
this epistolary affair that began in faith and humility and ended
in irony.

As crucial as Higginson's apparent willingness to promote new
artists was his assertion that the public decides the lasting value
of poetry. "It is this vast, unimpassioned, unconscious tribunal,
this average judgment of intelligent minds, which is truly formidable, — something more undying than senates and more omnipotent than courts, something which rapidly cancels all transitory reputations, and at last becomes the organ of eternal justice
and infallibly awards posthumous fame." [17] The necessity for
public reading of one's work is persuasively, even if mostly emotionally, put, and in part the argument may have impelled Emily
Dickinson's response. Higginson's florid celebration of language
which may become "so saturated with warm life and delicious

association that every sentence shall palpitate and thrill with the mere fascination of the syllables" [18] is undoubtedly the particular line to which she referred when she asked in her first letter if her verse "breathed."

Their sharing of an effusive reverence for the poetic art also contributed to the evocative effect of the article. Higginson's regal metaphors mirror Emily Dickinson's own manner of characterizing the high station of achieved artistry. He admonishes his reader not to "undertake to exercise these prerogatives of royalty until you are quite sure of being crowned." [19] The image palls, as does his pronouncement that "a book is the only immortality." [20] But the statements sanctioned her vague identification of spiritual and literary immortality. They affirmed her recurrently implied belief that perhaps a literary afterlife still lay accessible beyond a world that denied assurance of salvation. Moreover, since Emily Dickinson was already a letter writer of some brilliance, no other exclamation could so firmly have bound her spirit to Higginson's and encouraged her initiation of a correspondence as the passage in which the man of letters proclaimed that "few men in all their pride of culture can emulate the easy grace of a bright woman's letter." [21]

The merit of Higginson's ideas aside, his invitation worked its professed intention. Undercut by the patronizing tone, his encouragement and offer of understanding yet survived to overcome the inhibitions of the private poet. Perhaps, too, his well-known radical feminism seemed to her to promise a properly receptive ground of appreciation.[22] The crusading attitude would appeal not only to the woman but also to the poet who knew herself to be an innovator in versification. Indeed, six weeks before her first letter to Higginson the early version of "Safe in their Alabaster Chambers" appeared in the *Springfield Daily Republican* (March 1, 1862). She included, in its revised form, that brilliantly compressed tracery of the circle of life and death and fearful conjecture on immortality in the group of four poems which she sent to Higginson in her first letter. In this coincidence of events and chance intersection of strangely divergent personalities the world had beckoned to the poet.[23] She did not ignore the occasion, for the world as she knew it rarely proffered this sort of hospitality.

The earliest letters in her long correspondence with Higginson embody Emily Dickinson's seemingly contradictory attitudes toward her ability and toward the craft of poetry. She sent six letters in the first year of their correspondence. They form, with the exception of the brief and irrelevant sixth letter (L–274), a coherent and useful body of personal commentary.[24] The constrained expression, issuing from an obsessively closed personality, startles us with its psychological disclosures. Most apparent in the five letters, aside from their implied purpose to find publication for the author's poetry, is a pervasive humility, an artlessness that seems to express the writer's self-regard. The first letter (L–260) is hesitant, pleading, the poet apparently confessing her inability to judge her own work. "The Mind is so near itself," she writes, "it cannot see, distinctly — and I have none to ask." She suggests that she is incapable of knowing whether or not the verses she has enclosed are indeed poetry, for she says, "If I make the mistake — that you dared to tell me — would give me sincerer honor — toward you." The "mistake," though one cannot be certain since it is nowhere defined, is probably the "dishonoring" of the poetic art by hasty composition and a rush for publication. In the *Atlantic Monthly* article Higginson had admonished: "Such being the majesty of the art you seek to practise, you can at least take time and deliberation before dishonoring it." [25] The line lodged in Emily Dickinson's mind, for fifteen years later she quoted it back to him (L–488). She may have been referring to other "mistakes," however. Higginson warns in the article not to be tedious, abstruse, commonplace, or mannered. He declares "symmetry" and "vigor" the ideal poetic attributes.[26]

In the second letter, dated April 25 (L–261), she says again that she is incapable of assessing her work: "While my thought is undressed — I can make the distinction, but when I put them [sic] in the Gown [of words] — they look alike, and numb." She attests apparently to only the briefest apprenticeship: "I made no verse — but one or two — until this winter — Sir." Further on she declares her novitiate: "I would like to learn — Could you tell me how to grow — or is it unconveyed — like Melody — or Witchcraft?" She implies that her verses serve a childish need for manufactured courage: "I sing, as the Boy does by the Burying Ground — because I am afraid." In the next letter, dated June 7 (L–265), she humbly disavows any intent to publish: "I smile when you suggest I delay 'to publish' — that being foreign to my thought, as Firmament to Fin." And she asks again for instruction: "If I might bring you what I do — not so frequent to trouble you — and ask you if I told it clear — 'twould be control, to me."

The fourth letter, dated July (L–268), maintains the pose of the ingénue. She seems still to be beset by a sense of her own awkwardness. "An ignorance, not of Customs, but if caught with the Dawn — or the Sunset see me — Myself the only Kangaroo among the Beauty, Sir, if you please, it afflicts me," she pleads, "and I thought that instruction would take it away." She declares her ignorance again in the fifth letter, dated August (L–271): "You say I confess the little mistake, and omit the large — Because I can see Orthography — but the Ignorance out of sight — is my Preceptor's charge." In closing, she declares: "I shall observe your precept — though I don't understand it, always."

The persistent self-effacement seems the monologue of one pitifully small and ridiculous. The tone contrasts sharply, however, with that in a letter (L–269), to her friends the Hollands, for example, written at about the same time.[27] Significantly, the poet refers to a singer in her garden who performs but has no audience. "Perhaps," she writes, "the whole United States are laughing at me too! I can't stop for that! *My* business is to love.

I found a bird, this morning, down – down – on a little bush at the foot of the garden, and wherefore sing, I said, since nobody *hears?*" This confident self-regard lies masked in the letters to Higginson. It not only makes her correspondence the dramatic expression of an intricate personality; it gives the lie to her pose. The evidence takes different forms. Her letters for the most part are extremely mannered. The forced style is not alien to her habitual way; rather, it studiously avoids compromising her unique, often cryptic, mode of expression. One feels she was intent upon demonstrating to him the ways of an extraordinary woman. The mannerism obtrudes most noticeably where her prose turns abruptly into metered expression. In the third letter (L–265), for example, she writes:

> I have a little shape–it would not crowd your
> Desk–nor make much Racket as the Mouse, that
> dents your Galleries–
> If I might bring you what I do–not so frequent
> to trouble you–and ask you if I told it clear–
> 'twould be control, to me–
> The Sailor cannot see the North–but knows the
> Needle can–

Similar versified expression reappears in her fifth letter (L–271): "I had no Monarch in my life, and cannot rule myself, and when I try to organize – my little Force explodes – and leaves me bare and charred –." The rhythms of poetry, she seems to be demonstrating, so pervade her consciousness that she cannot make the distinction between them and unmetered prose. She allows the poetic impulse to intrude even as she is declaring her artlessness.

She makes a remarkable offering of information for one to whom the thought of publishing is supposed to be utterly foreign. In her second letter she writes: "Two Editors of Journals came to my Father's House, this Winter – and asked me for my Mind – and when I asked them 'Why,' they said I was penurious – and they, would use it for the World" (L–261). The editors were probably her friends Samuel Bowles, the famous editor of the *Springfield Daily Republican* from 1851 until his death, and Josiah Gilbert Holland, an associate of Bowles on the Springfield paper, in 1870 the founder of *Scribner's Monthly*, and generally popular man of letters.[28] If the assumption is correct, the fact that Emily Dickinson portrays these two close friends so abstractly suggests she may have been marshaling authority to impress her reader. More important, however, Emily Dickinson had here injected into the correspondence the clear idea of publication.

Higginson must have asked her to explain her cryptic language in the poems and letters. She writes in the fifth letter (L–271): "All men say 'What' to me, but I thought it a fashion." The tone of this reply is imperious and uncompromising. Ironically, in her refusal to accommodate Higginson with an explication, she followed his own advice in the *Atlantic Monthly* article not to "waste a minute, not a second, in trying to demonstrate to others the merit of your own performance. If your work does not vindicate itself, you cannot vindicate it."[29] She pursued that unbending attitude throughout her life. It was her defense against intrusion by uncongenial minds.

The bold disregard of prosodic convention in the first poems she offered attests also to the strength of her sense of independence. She took Higginson at his word when he declared in his article that "every editor is always hungering and thirsting after novelties."[30] Three of the first four poems she sent him were in wayward metrical forms. The four poems were "Safe in their Alabaster Chambers" (P–216), "The nearest Dream recedes– unrealized–" (P–319), "We play at Paste" (P–320), and "I'll tell you how the Sun rose" (P–318).[31] Of the four, only the last follows regular form, being a variation on common hymn meter. No consistent syllabic pattern operates in the other three, and stress patterns shift from two to six in a line. In "Safe in their Alabaster Chambers," for example, the syllabic count ranges

irregularly from eleven to four. The stress pattern shifts from
two to six in a line. Of the two occasions of rhyme in the thirteen
lines, only one is exact. Obviously the poet made little concession
to current taste in the first gathering she made from her store of
poems. She was encouraged in her choice by the wording in the
critic's article, encouraged even to represent her work by a
greater proportion of irregularly formed verses than in fact
existed in the whole of her work to that date. She demonstrated
a conscious sophistication credible only in a person whose personal sense of artistic maturity is firmly held. Higginson's response cannot have been enthusiastic. In her first reply to him,
in comment upon his criticism of the four poems he had read,
she writes: "Thank you for the surgery — it was not so painful
as I supposed. I bring you others — as you ask — though they
might not differ." (Ironically, in the line preceding she says she
is recuperating: "Your kindness claimed earlier gratitude — but I
was ill — and write today, from my pillow.") After the first letter
to Higginson, Emily Dickinson did not again presume to tax his
critical patience with wayward verse.

The assurance she contrived to hide is also revealed in the
daring simplicity of the arguments of two poems. "We play at
Paste" (P–320), accompanying the first letter, declares a recognition of her accomplishment in the most undisguised terms:

> We play at Paste–
> Till qualified, for Pearl–
> Then, drop the Paste–
> And deem ourself a fool–
>
> The Shapes–though–were similar–
> And our new Hands
> Learned *Gem*-Tactics–
> Practicing *Sands*–

The "*Gem*-Tactics," we may assume, represent the facility with
which Emily Dickinson, in her maturing skill, edged her brittle
language with a lapidary's precision. "Pearl" signifies poetic ac-

complishment arrived at after years of apprenticeship. She sent a second poem of this sort (P–326) in her fifth letter. It exploits the ballet metaphor with which it begins: "I cannot dance upon my Toes." The poet here was, in the single poem, both seeming to confirm her preceptor's low assessment of her ability and affirming her own awareness of a mature talent. Her apparent acquiescence in Higginson's opinion provides the initial tone:

> I cannot dance upon my Toes–
> No Man instructed me–
> But oftentimes, among my mind,
> A Glee possesseth me,
>
> That had I Ballet knowledge–
> Would put itself abroad
> In Pirouette to blanch a Troupe–
> Or lay a Prima, mad.

The contrary attitude, the clear notice of possession of the artistic faculty — together with disdain for the mannerisms which pass for fine performance in a theater concerned with frills — charges the closing stanzas. Though not a public performer, she says, her "Art" is filled to capacity:

> And though I had no Gown of Gauze–
> No Ringlet, to my Hair,
> Nor hopped for Audiences–like Birds,
> One Claw upon the Air,
>
> Nor tossed my shape in Eider Balls,
> Nor rolled on wheels of snow
> Till I was out of sight, in sound,
> The House encore me so–
>
> Nor any know I know the Art
> I mention–easy–Here–
> Nor any Placard boast me–
> It's full as Opera–

This speaker, contemptuous even as she vividly describes the costumes and gestures on the public stage, possesses more than a faint regard for her own ability. The poet realized that Higginson was baffled by her extraordinary performance, yet she neither wanted to malign his critical intelligence nor minimize her own talents.

Like the bold tone of the two poems on the craft of poetry and the independence reflected in her choice of unconventional poems in the first letters, another characteristic of the work she sent him argues her feeling of achievement. The emotional tension in succeeding poems rises in effective crescendo. She probes progressively deeper into psychic turmoil. Higginson suggested she was "spasmodic" (she answered pointedly in her third letter: "You think my gait 'spasmodic' — I am in danger — Sir —"); her poems show that her allegiance to her own conception of her art overrode his critical clichés. She enabled him to witness the extent of her exploration of the mind's terror whether or not he was to question its decorum.

The increasing emotional tautness informs three poems. In her first letter she enclosed "The nearest Dream recedes–unrealized" (P–319), the burden of the statement being that the deepest kind of desire, that for spiritual salvation, is precisely the one that is denied any anticipatory sign of fulfillment. The intensity of the feeling sharpens from the bland and playful invitation at the opening to the climax where the pursuer is callously mocked by universal indifference:

> The nearest Dream recedes–unrealized–
> The Heaven we chase,
> Like the June Bee–before the School Boy,
> Invites the Race–
> Stoops–to an easy Clover–
> Dips–evades–teazes–deploys–
> Then–to the Royal Clouds
> Lifts his light Pinnace–
> Heedless of the Boy–
> Staring–bewildered–at the mocking sky–
>
> Homesick for steadfast Honey–

By the closing two lines we have come beyond simple disappointment to an attitude of tragic resignation:

> Ah, the Bee flies not
> That brews that rare variety!

The heedless world is the more hideous for working its deceit on the innocent and credulous child.[32] The skepticism hardly mirrored Higginson's cozy faith in heavenly rewards for those who live nobly day by day.

Her second letter enclosed "There came a Day at Summer's full" (P–322). The metaphor of the double crucifixion embodies the intricate agony of the encounter between ill-fated lovers. The tone is resonant with the devotional cadences of the sacrament of the faithful.

> The time was scarce profaned, by speech–
> The symbol of a word
> Was needless, as at Sacrament,
> The Wardrobe–of our Lord–
>
> Each was to each The Sealed Church,
> Permitted to commune this–time–
> Lest we too awkward show
> At Supper of the Lamb.
>
> The Hours slid fast–as Hours will,
> Clutched tight, by greedy hands–
> So faces on two Decks, look back,
> Bound to opposing lands–
>
> And so when all the time had leaked,
> Without external sound
> Each bound the Other's Crucifix–
> We gave no other Bond–
>
> Sufficient troth, that we shall rise–
> Deposed–at length, the Grave–
> To that new Marriage,
> Justified–through Calvaries of Love–

The promise of an eventual spiritual union competes momentarily but never overcomes the emphatic images of the emotional wrenching the speaker is resigned to suffering in an earthly purgatory of separations and sacrifices.

The third poem, "Of Tribulation–these are They" (P–325), declares with a terrible simplicity the private triumph over despair. Its power derives from the image of the exhausted runner on the darkened road. The stark language, unimpeded by tricks of rhetoric, offers simultaneously the expression of stoical endurance, the anguish and fear, and finally the clear affirmative exclamation of the final achievement of the goal:

> Of Tribulation–these are They,
> Denoted by the White.
> The Spangled Gowns, a lesser Rank
> Of Victors, designate–
>
> All these–did conquer–
> But the Ones who overcame most times–
> Wear nothing commoner than Snow–
> No Ornament–but Palms–
>
> "Surrender"–is a sort unknown
> On this Superior soil–
> "Defeat", an Outgrown Anguish,
> Remembered–as the Mile
>
> Our panting An[k]le barely passed,
> When Night devoured the Road–
> But we–stood–whispering in the House–
> And all we said–was
> > > SAVED!

The psychological disclosures in these three poems startle us by their directness. They convey the obsessive quality of very personal intensities. One sees in them an unflinching confrontation with anguish maturing into an acceptance of life's denials. Higginson might fatuously wag "spasmodic," when indeed the po-

etry takes us dramatically beyond clichés of anguish and emotional indulgence to the firm ground of private courage.

Where Higginson's complacency betrayed him, of course, was
in his notion that current taste and convention constitute poetic
merit. Emily Dickinson's wry notification that "All men say
'What' to me, but I thought it a fashion" announced her awareness of her superiority and her unwillingness to compromise her
vision to meet the questionable demands of contemporary taste.
Her confident attitude, contrary to her pose of artlessness, is
perfectly consistent with the other less obvious tendencies discernible in the first year's correspondence. The unique rhetoric
of the letters constitutes a stylistic declaration of independence.
The unconventional poems she first sent the editor who professed to thirst after novelty demonstrate her confidence in her
own experimentation. The verses on the subject of poetry demonstrate that she felt knowledgeable enough as an artist to speak on
the artist's craft. The intensity of the poetically rendered emotion
she was willing for her correspondent to witness demonstrates
her desire to exhibit the range of her capabilities. And, finally,
her sense of her maturity as a poet is implicit in the unmistakable
desire for publication which her letters to Higginson in 1862
document. In her own mind certainly, the formative period had
by then reached an end.

ASPIRATION AND ITS

ANALOGUES

We find thorough justification of Emily Dickinson's confidence as an artist in her poetic performance of the early period. To judge the merit of that performance and specifically to illuminate her frequently cryptic expression, it is necessary first to discover her controlling thematic concern, the matrix from which the poems spring. Recognition of that major theme is essential, for otherwise there is scanty narrative context to provide referents for the equivocal symbolic values in the imagery of much of her poetry. This apparent ambiguity has contributed to a judgment that the poet often wrote out of an intense anguish so private that the reader must necessarily be denied understanding. Yet equally common is the judgment that her poetry provides delight, that is, that it effectively communicates. When G. F. Whicher speaks of the "peculiar fascination" of Emily Dickinson's poetry, he is suggesting the disparity between enjoyment and understanding, between the imaginative power of the poetry and its evasion of precise critical rendering.[1] The poetry makes adequate critical comment more difficult than usual.

Thoughtful readers of Emily Dickinson's poetry have pursued a variety of approaches to the body of work in an effort to discover coherence, so that the poetry may be discussed within some sort of rational framework. Jay Leyda argues that one of the first necessities is to find "a major theme or continuity in the poems." [2] Whether there is an organizing principle to be found, or whether each poem is a fragment, and the canon a random scattering of fragments out of which one is free to make his own mosaic, constitutes the fundamental problem. The first effort, generally, of the critical mind when confronted with the numerous poems is to reduce their meanings to a set of rational categories. For a few critics, however, the reverse is true: the cohering principle is judged to be simply the fact that no principle inheres, that the character of the body of poetry is best described as chaotic. Louis Untermeyer, for example, implies that whatever coherence the poems may have lies in the enigmatic private turmoil of Emily Dickinson's mind. Of the poems he declares: "The few lines became telegraphic and these telegrams seemed not only self-addressed but written in code."[3] If they have any coherence as a group, he suggests, it lies in the fact that they are "the notes for her uncoordinated autobiography."[4] R. P. Blackmur says in effect much the same, but he does not retreat to the biographical principle to account for the apparent fragmentation of the body of work. "She never undertook," he says, "the great profession of controlling the means of objective expression. That is why the bulk of her verse is not representative but mere fragmentary indicative notation."[5]

But if for some readers the mind's impulse is to accept the seemingly chaotic principle of the poems, to resist imposing what they believe to be a delusive fixity upon the thematic direction of the poems, there are others who attempt to define a core element to which the works relate. The reading of Yvor Winters is sympathetic on the whole, for he concludes that Emily Dickinson is one of the greatest lyric poets of all time; yet his critical judgment polarizes about what seems to him to be a pervasive weakness in the canon. "The quality of silly playfulness," he writes, ". . . is diffused more or less perceptibly throughout most of her work, and this diffusion is facilitated by the limited range of her metrical schemes."[6] In Winters' critique we recognize a rephrasing of that ambivalent attitude which characterizes much of the response to Emily Dickinson's poetry. If it is a lack of seriousness on which Winters fixes, it is the inscrutability that draws the attention of Leyda. The organizing principle, Leyda believes, derives from an apparently perverse crypticism, a playful and deliberate obscurity on the part of the poet. He finds in the incomprehensibility of the poems their defining character: "A major device of Emily Dickinson's writing, both in her poems and in her letters, was what might be called the 'omitted center.' The riddle, the circumstance too well known to be repeated to the initiate, the deliberate skirting of the obvious — this was the means she used to increase the privacy of her communication; it has also increased our problems in piercing that privacy." [7]

In his incisive study of Emily Dickinson's poetry, Richard Chase finds at the core of the writing the single idea of status. This view is helpful precisely to the extent to which status is *not defined*. Chase writes: "In Emily Dickinson's poetry, taking it by and large, there is but one major theme, one symbolic act, one incandescent center of meaning. Expressed in the most general terms, this theme is the achievement of status through crucial experiences." [8] As a general statement of the central theme which engages Emily Dickinson, Chase's description serves. It is particularly useful because it encompasses the sense of the intense pressure of certain experiences represented in the poems, experiences, indeed, which illuminate the conditions of aspiration and achievement. Chase attempts, however, to fix precisely this central orientation of the poet's mind, and in so doing excludes from his definition a considerable body of her poetry. "The central trope of Emily Dickinson's poems," he declares, "could be said to be similar to the myth of Cinderella, if in the fairy tale the marriage is with death and 'living happily ever after' referred to eternity." [9] But the immortality which Emily Dickinson envisions does not at all times mesh with Christian orthodoxy. It tends, at times, to be analogue for the ultimate condition of the completed personality. For Emily Dickinson, the ultimate realization of the emotions is love, and the ultimate fulfillment of her poetic capabilities is the literary immortality contingent upon poetic achievement.

Thomas H. Johnson, like Chase, defines the characteristic tendency of the poet's mind as a quest for assurance — in particular, for assurance of achievement of a timeless afterlife: "Lurking behind every thought to which she gave expression was the abiding wonder, the craving for assurance, about the sempiternal." [10] We know, however, that this definition of the major continuity in the poems excludes the sharp awareness of the present and the intensely vital earthly experience which inform such poems as "I taste a liquor never brewed" (P–214), "She sweeps with many-colored Brooms" (P–219), "I can wade Grief" (P–252), "Delight is as the flight" (P–257), "The Robin's my Criterion for Tune" (P–285), and "Of Bronze–and Blaze" (P–290).

The opposing approach, which groups poems according to various subject matter, imposes its own sort of limitation on the possible readings. The earliest classification, that of Higginson and Mabel Loomis Todd, the first editors, persists and serves to separate the poems into groups which apparently deal with Life, Love, Nature, Time, and Eternity. Charles Anderson suggests that ecstasy and despair, death and immortality, represent major thematic concerns: "The dramatic poles of human existence, Ecstasy and Despair, [are] two themes that produced far better poems than any of the more moderate aspects of the inner life. Finally, since ecstasy and despair are inextricably related to spiritual strivings and misgivings, they lead inevitably to her thematic concern with man's knowledge of Death and his dream of Immortality." [11] But those who fragment the canon and arrange the poems under arbitrary metaphysical headings Leyda regards rightly as serving to promote the sentimental picture of Emily Dickinson in which her poems seem to be "discrete, discontinuous little snatches from infinity." [12]

Of these three approaches to an ordering of the poems — the approach which accepts them on their face as chaotic and isolated impulses, the approach which attempts to confine the poems within a single and limited idea, and the approach which separates them into categories of subjects (effecting a form of fragmentation only slightly less chaotic than the first approach) — no single method serves satisfactorily as an organizing procedure. These approaches err in focusing too closely on the appearance of the poems (their brevity, their nondiscursive form), or they err in being shortsighted (concerned too hastily with subjects, the metaphorical or analogical constructs), or they maneuver outside the poems themselves for an organizing principle. This third method, which leads ultimately to the poet's personality, is, if not a last resort, certainly the path of least resistance, for lacking other clear guides one may simply rely on the fact that a single person composed the poems out of her own experience of self and the world.

It is particularly important in a consideration of Emily Dickinson's poetry to make as clear a distinction as possible between the controlling theme and the contexts in which that theme is expressed. For on the one hand, to suggest that a single *idea* controls her work is to impose a single reading on poems which are in fact abstract, equivocal in their symbolic meanings, and capable of more than one reading. On the other hand, to limit interpretation to the level of the subject matter, that is, to the contextual situation or analogue which manifests the controlling attitude, is to fragment the canon and ignore the cohering viewpoint which exists. The most revealing critical perspective we shall discover located in a middle distance.

The term *theme* I employ to denote the central and controlling disposition of the poet's mind as that particular tendency of mind determines what the poems are about. The subjects, on the other hand, are the various situations or contexts in which the theme is materialized or manifested. Death, for example, may be said to be the theme of Donne's "Death, be not proud," of Yeats's "An Irish Airman Foresees His Death," and of Frost's "The Death of the Hired Man," yet the contextual situations and attitudes are obviously different. An early example of Emily Dickinson's work in which the distinction becomes clear is "I have a Bird in spring" (P–5). In this poem the speaker ruminates on the disappearance of the robin which arrives early in the year to "decoy" spring into coming. As the poem proceeds, one finds that the seasonal situation from which the thoughts arise soon gives way to the controlling theme of separation, of parting from the spectacle of spring and from friends who go away. The poem becomes an objectification of human aspiration for reunion with what has been lost to time. The second stanza reads:

> Yet do I not repine
> Knowing that Bird of mine
> Though flown–
> Learneth beyond the sea
> Melody new for me
> And will return.

The object of the emotion here is still the robin who has departed. There is the vague belief that it leaves for other, perhaps mythical, lands from which it will bring again another spring and another song of inspiration. In the third and fourth stanzas, however, the contemplative mind reaches out uncertainly to embrace a vague host of wanderers:

> Fast in a safer hand
> Held in a truer Land
> Are mine–
> And though they now depart,
> Tell I my doubting heart
> They're thine.

> In a serener Bright,
> In a more golden light
> I see
> Each little doubt and fear,
> Each little discord here
> Removed.

"That Bird of mine," the initial object of feeling, fades into the pronoun "they," which has only the indefinite referent "mine" in the preceding line. Whatever departs has gone to a secure repose where the speaker herself believes she will find surcease from present discord, doubt, and fear.

The movement in this poem from the definite situation to the abstract theme is awkward because the speaker passes abruptly from the robin as object to an unidentified group of vagrant loves. However, *the state of mind expressed remains constant.* The emotional response to separation and the contemplation of reunion provide the basic theme which the poet objectifies in figures and form. The subject of the poem is, indeed, the passing of spring and of the robin, but this is merely the *subject* which makes manifest the lyrical meditation on vague, uncommitted desire.

From the five earliest poems various contextual situations embodying this controlling desire for fulfillment emerge. The first poem (P–1), which begins with a conventional plea to the muses, continues:

Oh the Earth was *made* for lovers, for damsel, and hopeless swain,
For sighing, and gentle whispering, and *unity* made of *twain.*

The piece is extended into an elaborate valentine, including a remarkable catalogue and argument in favor of the general condition in nature where unity is made of twain. The tone is whimsical, in keeping with the commonplace conventions of valentine pleadings, but the controlling theme is aspiration for fulfillment, for the achievement of oneness out of existing separation. The other four poems, though differing in tone and in the situations from which the expression arises, also deal with some form of separation. The second poem (P–2), included in a letter to her brother Austin while he was away at school, offers comfort to the student who was supposedly homesick. The third poem (P–3), a bright parody of bombastic political speeches, is in its own whimsical tone and macaronic manner a treatment of the condition of separation:

> Good bye, Sir, I am going;
>   My country calleth me;
> Allow me, Sir, at parting,
>   To wipe my weeping e'e.

The fourth poem (P–4) is a declaration of the love of the speaker, who will pilot the "thee" of the poem to eternity, where the two will find the repose impossible in their earthly state:

> In the peaceful west
> Many the sails at rest—
> The anchors fast—
> Thither I pilot *thee.*

Poem Five, discussed above, deals at its most significant dimension with separation from what time takes away.

The aspiring attitude appears with varying intensity, and coincident with that attitude is a sustaining tone (evident when the speaker identifies herself with the pilot figure in "On this wondrous sea" [P–4]), or a lighter and detached tone which relieves potentially grave situations of any profound emotional involvement. Melville's *Pierre*, published about the time of Emily Dickinson's earliest work (1852), employs the Enceladus figure, the earth-bound but aspiring individual, as one of its symbols; the figure is appropriate for the speaker in these early Dickinson poems. One must acknowledge without delay that the imagery in these earliest works is flatly conventional and the effect is the subordination of feeling to the conspicuous display of rhetorical versatility. The mode of expression, that is, seems to have engaged the poet more than the emotion.

In general, then, the disposition of Emily Dickinson's mind is between the poles of the *now* and the *hoped for*, between actuality and ideality. The act of the speaker's mind in her poetry is one of aspiration, of attempting to effect a bridge between the two poles. The poet's images of the seaborne looking for the shore, of the isolate seeking union and fulfillment, of the speaker sustaining those who are separated by geography or time (by distance or by death), persist. In the poems dated through 1861 the subjects vary widely; the theme of separation (of isolation, of the quest for union and fulfillment), however, recurs and controls. It represents, indeed, an obsessively persistent regard for the dark psychological underside of poetry of revelation and of the sort of spiritual rapture that we associate with the romantic temperament. Emily Dickinson apparently craved mental dissatisfaction, and in exploring the emotional heavings of this condition she re-mystified and made tragic again a world that in the glass of transcendentalism had become too cozy and familiar. Her excursions kept turning inward and, in Keats's words, unlike the ancient poets whose provinces were vast she, like an Elector of Hanover, governed her petty state, and knew how many straws were daily swept.[13] The tension in her poetry derives from this unrelenting contemplation of the dilemma of isolation and the necessity of human love.

The 1858 poems reassert the poet's central concern with the active effort of the mind to overcome disparity. Among these works and those of the other early years are several poems apparently written with the specific purpose of sending them to friends. The greater part of these occasional pieces are the products of Emily Dickinson's participation in the sentimental cult of her time.[14] Significantly, however, they represent the least dramatic and most conventional dimension of her theme; in them union is to be effected by the bonds of friendship. An exception is the poem beginning "If she had been the Mistletoe" (P–44).[15] Subdued but still apparent is the act, however facetiously treated, of aspiring to a close association:

> If she had been the Mistletoe
> And I had been the Rose–
> How gay upon your table
> My velvet life to close–
> Since I am of the Druid,
> And she is of the dew–
> I'll deck Tradition's buttonhole–
> And send the Rose to you.

Beneath the surface concern for making a pleasantry and a flattering declaration of affection, the poem deals centrally with the speaker's own regard for herself. She recognizes that her isolated condition is unalterable. To what tradition she is committed is not clear; perhaps this higher calling is poetic dedication and the writer is aware that the poetic impulse works through her ("Since I am of the Druid") and that it makes her different from others. What interests us in this poem, however, is the acknowledged condition of separation (reductive analogue of the ultimate separation of death) together with the fact that this theme arises from the apparently whimsical material of a declaration of friendship.

In another poem dated 1858, one finds the poet confronting the *ultimate* form of separation, *death*. In "When I count the seeds" (P–40) the attention turns inward and the progression of the poet's thought travels from the analytical to the intuitive:

> When I count the seeds
> That are sown beneath,
> To bloom so, bye and bye–
>
> When I con the people
> Lain so low,
> To be received as high–

When I believe the garden
Mortal shall not see—
Pick by faith it's blossom
And avoid it's Bee,
I can spare this summer, unreluctantly.

The subtle alteration of verbs which trace the more inward movement is crucial. In the first stanza the verb is analytical, that is, the speaker sees in the analogy of the seed that is to bloom later the process of resurrection (the dead "Lain so low" will be "received as high"). In the second stanza the verb becomes *con*, the attempt to understand, and the object remains the process by which the dead are resurrected. The mode of thought has shifted from rational inquiry to contemplation in which one's own emotions are committed. In the final stanza, we note the verb changes to *believe*, the implication being that only by faith can one turn away with assurance from the present joys of summer and of this life to the afterlife. Only by faith, that is, can one confront the mystery (and perhaps painful fact) of death which constitutes the passage from conjecture to knowing. The poem recreates the inward turning of the speaker's mind and the inner dialogue which, beginning in objectivity and taking note of the fact of death and the fact of regeneration in nature, ends in a recognition that ultimately faith determines whether or not one accepts the truth of nature's analogue of the resurrection which the buried seeds represent.

A major part of Emily Dickinson's poetry in the formative years weighs this anticipation of fulfillment, of a safe repose, of reunion, of achievement. Another considerable part of her poetry deals with the bridging of the polar situations. This group is concerned with the observable *process* by which one passes from the *here* to the *conjectured*. In the final sense this process is death and resurrection. "There's something quieter than sleep" (P–45) is representative of the many instances when the poet's attention turned to the fact of death as the precise moment of transition:

There's something quieter than sleep
Within this inner room!
It wears a sprig upon it's breast–
And will not tell it's name.

Some touch it, and some kiss it–
Some chafe it's idle hand–
It has a simple gravity
I do not understand!

I would not weep if I were they–
How rude in one to sob!
Might scare the quiet fairy
Back to her native wood!

While simple-hearted neighbors
Chat of the "Early dead"–
We–prone to periphrasis,
Remark that Birds have fled!

It is not surprising that many critics have concluded that death is the central and morbid concern of Emily Dickinson. Poems such as this one seem to support the contention. One must recognize, however, that in this poet's mind the idea of death is repeatedly accompanied by the idea of the *possibility* of life after death. Death is the bridge which must be crossed, and in itself, therefore, it warrants specific attention.[16] In many poems, such as this one, the tone is clearly not one of morbidity. "There's something quieter than sleep," indeed, is defiantly pert. The speaker describes the conventional reaction to death: "Some chafe it's idle hand." The mourners conduct themselves as if they understood the experience of death. The speaker, however, declares candidly of the corpse: "It has a simple gravity / I do not understand!" And so, rather than chatting conventionally of the "Early dead," she evades the subject and speaks laconically (and certainly ironically, since the declaration is anything but periphrastic) of the birds that have fled. The result, of course, is that having begun with the conventional responses

to death the poem shifts to a shockingly unconventional tone,
becoming in its rejection of convention an anti-threnody. It
places death not in an horrendous role but simply as the brief
inscrutable process between this life and another. Death mysti-
fies us, she implies, but neither more nor less than the familiar
migration of the birds.

Several other early poems scrutinize the gestures the living
make in the act of death. The perspective is almost clinical, re-
minding one of Hans Castorp's early experience of death in *The
Magic Mountain.* Thomas Mann writes:

At the bier he displayed both an uncomprehending coolness and a
detached alertness of observation, to which were added . . . a feeling and expression of connoisseurship. And something more, a peculiar, precocious variation: he seemed no longer to think of tears–either
the frequent outburst of grief or the contagion from the grief of
others–as a natural reaction. In the three or four months after his
father's passing he had forgotten about death; but now he remembered, and all the impressions of that time recurred, precise, immediate, and piercing in their transcendant strangeness.[17]

Emily Dickinson found more in nature than analogues of
death and resurrection, however, and more than a useful syntax
to convey the self's silent questionings. Several early poems are
concerned principally with nature as spectacle, delightful of
itself. One of her earliest poems of this type sketches the drama
of a sunset and employs the device of personification that appears in much of her work. In "I never told the buried gold"
(P–11), she pictures the lowering sun as Captain Kidd burying
gold beneath the horizon, with the speaker a concealed specta-
tor, awed at the splendor and at the mystery. Other less familiar
nature poems are also primarily imagistic. The sunset is personified in "The Guest is gold and crimson" (P–15):

> The Guest is gold and crimson–
> An Opal guest and gray–
> Of Ermine is his doublet–
> His Capuchin gay.

The sunset is again her subject in "How the old Mountains drip with Sunset" (P–291), the first stanza of which reads:

> How the old Mountains drip with Sunset
> How the Hemlocks burn–
> How the Dun Brake is draped in Cinder
> By the Wizard Sun.

A winter snowfall is the subject of the early poem entitled "Snow flakes" (P–36):

> I counted till they danced so
> Their slippers leaped the town,
> And then I took a pencil
> To note the rebels down.
> And then they grew so jolly
> I did resign the prig,
> And ten of my once stately toes
> Are marshalled for a jig!

In "A Lady red–amid the Hill" (P–74), the poet's subject is the expectant mood pervading nature in the days before spring:

> A Lady red–amid the Hill
> Her annual secret keeps!
> A Lady white, within the Field
> In placid Lily sleeps!
>
> The tidy Breezes, with their Brooms–
> Sweep vale–and hill–and tree!
> Prithee, My pretty Housewives!
> Who may expected be?

The more familiar early works in this group of nature poems include "She sweeps with many-colored Brooms" (P–219), and "An awful Tempest mashed the air" (P–198), which begins:

> An awful Tempest mashed the air–
> The clouds were gaunt, and few–
> A Black–as of a Spectre's Cloak
> Hid Heaven and Earth from View.[18]

What relationship do such works have with the thematic focus of the early years? Emily Dickinson's imagistic nature poems reflect her central theme as they imply the ideal in nature — brilliant color, harmony, spring following the sleep of winter, or, as in Poem 198, the calm following a storm. Sometimes they treat the natural world as the affirmative yet indecipherable ceremony of a purposeful creation. The clearest expression in the early poems of the ritualistic quality in nature which evokes in the poet a vision of triumph over isolation occurs in "A something in a summer's Day" (P–122). The appropriate stanzas are the opening two:

> A something in a summer's Day
> As slow her flambeaux burn away
> Which solemnizes me.
>
> A something in a summer's noon–
> A depth–an Azure–a perfume–
> Transcending extasy.

Yet the poet is not consistently so assured of the promise in natural ritual, for she displays an awareness in "Make me a picture of the sun" (P–188) that one may subjectively choose from the show of nature only those gestures which beckon comfortingly. The observer, she implies partly through her use of quotation marks here, assigns her own values to what she sees. The final stanza of the poem reads:

> Say if it's really–warm at noon–
> Whether it's Buttercups–that "skim"–
> Or Butterflies–that "bloom"?
> Then–skip–the frost–upon the lea–
> And skip the Russet–on the tree–
> Let's play those–never come!

The poet acknowledges her separation from nature. She is once more aware that the aspiration for understanding must be denied satisfaction.[19]

More central evidence of the controlling theme in Emily Dickinson's early poetry is the poem "Some things that fly there be" (P–89). The elliptic expression contributes to the effectiveness of this piece, its stark simplicity giving fresh relevance to the conventional imagery. The poem's principal significance, however, is the characteristic attitude which it reveals. The movement of mind, as we saw in "There's something quieter than sleep," is away from the natural world to the intellectual, the lyrical meditation beginning in a perception of the facts of nature:

> Some things that fly there be–
> Birds–Hours–the Bumblebee–
> Of these no Elegy.
>
> Some things that stay there be–
> Grief–Hills–Eternity–
> Nor this behooveth me.
>
> There are that resting, rise.
> Can I expound the skies?
> How still the Riddle lies!

This poem is a particularly concise articulation of the theme that continually compelled the attention of the poet and dominates her works. The focus is on the quest of the speaker's mind for reconciliation of the paradoxes in nature and in the mind. The first stanza is a neat mixture of poetic whimsy and firm stoical attitude. The whimsy resides in the pun on *fly*: as birds and bumblebees soar in the air and disappear at the close of summer, the hours disappear in the passage of one's life. This, of course, is conventional lyric material — the things in nature and in one's own life which are lost to time. But for these things, the resolute speaker declares as she abandons the lyrical attitude, there will be no lament. The second stanza presents the reverse — the things that supposedly *stay*, objects and emotions and conjectured states that are not lost to time — grief, hills, eternity. The pun is in the word *stay*. *Stay* may be read not only in the sense that this conglomeration of emotion, natural analogy, and faith apparently exists eternally outside of time, but also in the sense that these objects of experience would seem to be consolation for what is lost. But even these immutables, the speaker says, do not sustain her completely, for there are those who somehow pass from the one state, the evanescent state of the first stanza, to the lasting state represented in the second stanza. Then more precisely, the third stanza presents the speculation that those who die do indeed fly up in resurrection into the eternal state of immortality. How, the speaker asks, does one make this bridge between time and eternity? Her answer is the exclamation, "How still the Riddle lies!"

One bridge is faith, as we saw in the poem "When I count the seeds." The dilemma is clear in "Some things that fly there be"; in its concisest form it is expressed in the paradoxical condition of those that "resting, rise," those who through death and resurrection make the transition from hours to eternity. The mind's activity within the riddle, between the poles of the actual and the conjectural, is the struggle to resolve the paradox. It is this struggle that Emily Dickinson articulates: the process of mind in its perpetual effort to reconcile and to unify, to bring to acceptable terms the perception of things that fly and things that stay.

In the poems dated 1859 and 1860, one finds the poet's attention drawn repeatedly to this theme. The poem "Just lost, when I was saved!" (P–160) places the speaker tensely within the area between the world and eternity:

> Just lost, when I was saved!
> Just felt the world go by!
> Just girt me for the onset with Eternity,
> When breath blew back,
> And on the other side
> I heard recede the disappointed tide!

Therefore, as One returned, I feel,
Odd secrets of the line to tell!
Some Sailor, skirting foreign shores–
Some pale Reporter, from the awful doors
Before the Seal!

Next time, to stay!
Next time, the things to see
By Ear unheard,
Unscrutinized by Eye–

Next time, to tarry,
While the Ages steal–
Slow tramp the Centuries,
And the Cycles wheel!

Having had an intuition of the "other side" through some crucial experience, perhaps sickness or bereavement (one cannot
know for certain), the speaker hopes for a permanent metamorphosis to that eternal state. The emotional response expresses
both wonderment and fear. But, characteristically of Emily
Dickinson, the vision escapes specific representation. It takes instead the vague form of intimations — "Odd secrets" — accompanying an unnamed but crucial experience. The disposition of
alternative conditions is clear; the process by which one makes
the transition between them may be profound emotional experience or death. The poet, we see, is that same explorer in search
of some frustratingly undefined goal. "All her life," R. P. Blackmur says, "she was looking for a subject, and the looking *was*
her subject — in life as in poetry." [20]

Poems dated 1861 also concentrate on the individual's incessant quest. The Enceladus situation becomes in one poem
(P–239) that of Tantalus. We see again the poet's essential
acceptance of the inaccessibility of fulfillment:

"Heaven"–is what I cannot reach!
The Apple on the Tree–
Provided it do hopeless–hang–
That–"Heaven" is–to Me!

The Color, on the Cruising Cloud–
The interdicted Land–
Behind the Hill–the House behind–
There–Paradise–is found!

Her teazing Purples–Afternoons–
The credulous–decoy–
Enamored–of the Conjuror–
That spurned us–Yesterday!

In the end, the poem, as do others in which the object of attention is not clearly named, symbolizes the act of aspiring. It formulates by homely analogy the experience of searching.[21]

When the poet turns inward exclusively, and closes her attention down on a particular aspect of this psychic struggle, the object of scrutiny is anguish, the experience she calls elsewhere the "vulgar grimace in the Flesh" (P–479). In "A *Wounded* Deer–leaps highest" (P–165), the speaker is in a declarative mood, but even so there is an urgency in this psychological disclosure:

A *Wounded* Deer–leaps highest–
I've heard the Hunter tell–
'Tis but the Extasy of *death*–
And then the Brake is still!

The *Smitten* Rock that gushes!
The *trampled* Steel that springs!
A Cheek is always redder
Just where the Hectic stings!

Mirth is the Mail of Anguish–
In which it Cautious Arm,
Lest anybody spy the blood
And "you're hurt" exclaim!

The speaker knows that internal turmoil is latent, as in the steel spring, and that it is powerful and capable of involuntary outward show. Concealing the anguish behind a comic mask provides the fiction by which private sufferers lead public lives.

Fulfillment, or the mere contemplation of it, whether through love or through achievement of spiritual or literary immortality, raises the most intense pleasure. In such an expression as "Come slowly–Eden!" (P–211) one finds the speaker at some midpoint between control and complete abandonment:

> Come slowly–Eden!
> Lips unused to Thee–
> Bashful–sip thy Jessamines–
> As the fainting Bee–
>
> Reaching late his flower,
> Round her chamber hums–
> Counts his nectars–
> Enters–and is lost in Balms.

The goal is only vaguely suggested by the Eden metaphor and the flower simile. We feel acutely, however, the speaker's precarious balance between ecstatic anticipation and fear of a consuming passion. She pleads that the joy come at a pace to which she can accommodate. Combined here are complex tides of emotion which elsewhere flow singly, as in "A *Wounded* Deer–leaps highest" and "A transport one cannot contain" (P–184). Self-possessed at times, overwhelmed emotionally at others, aspiring and fearing, desiring and renouncing — these are the varied contextual attitudes through which is conveyed the central theme of the quest for fulfillment. The poet engaged her theme repeatedly, examining it in accordance with particular emotional states, and on occasion, as in "Come slowly–Eden!" recreating a tense combination of them. As Richard Wilbur has suggested, Emily Dickinson is "consistent in her concerns but inconsistent in her attitudes." [22] Most often, we see her goals inevitably discounted in the surpassing investment of desire.

In other poems from this period the poet explores with impressive insight the psychic defenses against anguish and the manner in which grief destroys the mind. "I can wade Grief" (P–252) asserts that the experience of pain creates the strength to confront new pain, and that the pressure of this countering effort is so powerful that if the weight of anguish is suddenly removed, like the sudden opening of a door, the interior pressure bursts out and the person is reduced to stumbling and unaccustomed awkwardness:

> I can wade Grief–
> Whole Pools of it–
> I'm used to that–
> But the least push of Joy
> Breaks up my feet–
> And I tip–drunken–
> Let no Pebble–smile–
> 'Twas the New Liquor–
> That was all!
>
> Power is only Pain–
> Stranded, thro' Discipline,
> Till Weights–will hang–
> Give Balm–to Giants–
> And they'll wilt, like Men–
> Give Himmaleh–
> They'll Carry–Him!

The final pronoun refers back to "Himmaleh," the poet's metaphor for grief. Giants under the weight of mountains will develop power from that pain. Given the balm of less strenuous labors, even giants will grow faint. The poem argues, characteristically, that emotional strength is not an inherent quality, but rather one created in the experience of anguish.

In one of Emily Dickinson's great poems, the speaker succumbs to her anguish and is thrown into psychic breakdown. This experience is recreated in the poem "I felt a Funeral, in my Brain" (P–280). Beginning with the particularly apt imagery of the interior wake, objectifying the inner grief, one hears the rending sounds of grief uninterruptedly, so intense, as the speaker says, that one can no longer discriminate among the senses. The entire body has become an ear:

> I felt a Funeral, in my Brain,
> And Mourners to and fro
> Kept treading–treading–till it seemed
> That Sense was breaking through–
>
> And when they all were seated,
> A Service, like a Drum–
> Kept beating–beating–till I thought
> My Mind was going numb–
>
> And then I heard them lift a Box
> And creak across my Soul
> With those same Boots of Lead, again,
> Then Space–began to toll,
>
> As all the Heavens were a Bell,
> And Being, but an Ear,
> And I, and Silence, some strange Race
> Wrecked, solitary, here–

In the final stanza, restored now in the Johnson edition, the mind gives way beneath the weight of the anguish:

> And then a Plank in Reason, broke,
> And I dropped down, and down–
> And hit a World, at every plunge,
> And Finished knowing–then.

The silent plunging down and the immensity of the descent, as if the victim were hurled headlong through the universe, effectively terminates the persistent sound images. To be "Finished knowing" is simultaneously to see the utter depths of one's despair where no new experience of grief is possible, and also to lose the faculty of knowing at all, to have one's mind disintegrate.

This dark response to the grief which irrevocable separation evokes is but one experience Emily Dickinson creates out of the contemplation of her theme. We should not expect an unvarying

attitude in her work, for if anything marks the poetry and makes
it unique it is her characteristic swing and poise between joy
and despair, between faith and skepticism, and between desire
and fear. The possibility of love, she writes in P–673, "invites–
appalls–endows– / Flits–glimmers–proves–dissolves– / Returns–
suggests–convicts–enchants." Her attitudes represent the diverse
feelings through which the poet engaged her central theme. That
theme is not the abstraction death or immortality or love or fame,
but rather the *act* of the mind in quest of all of these. For emotional longing, the ideal is love. For the poetic faculty, the ideal
is literary achievement. For the spirit's aspiration, the ideal is
immortality. We may go further than this to see that Emily
Dickinson is often inexplicit in identifying the particular object
of aspiration. The goals tend to fuse in unelaborated imagery of
journeys, of light, of marriage. Indeed, in later poems we find
a free substitution of *love* and *faith* (P–491) or *wifehood* and
immortality (P–461). What sentimentality remains may be
traced in part to the convention of sensibility informing the
poetry and lesser art of letter-writing in mid-nineteenth-century
New England.

The fragmentation of her poetic utterances may now reveal its
rationale. Emily Dickinson's essential artistry lies partly in con-
structing the sharp, nondiscursive image, the instant's insight
committed to language. For the momentary insight to be ex-
panded to discursive magnitude is to be false to the impulse. Gay
Wilson Allen finds historical sanction for this apparent fragmentation in the literary contexts of the periods before and after
Emily Dickinson. Her poetic style, he concludes, "is ejaculatory,
suggestive rather than completely formed, and it is perhaps in
this respect most of all that she is a link between Emerson and
the 'Imagists.'" [23] Beyond the historical sanction lies the poetic
temper, very modern in its assumptions, that eschews false shows
of oneness in a universe where discontinuity seems the only
trustworthy observation and where only provisional aggregations

of fragments convey meaning and protect the observer from self-destroying doubt.[24]

Emily Dickinson's habitual choice of *renunciation*, embodied everywhere in her theme, also reflects a familiar modern outlook. We find the easy achievement avoided as often in modern poetry as in modern art. In the culture from which this art springs, says Ernst Gombrich, "renunciation of gratification, nobility, and the good converge and become one."[25] But this attitude, too, has its provenance in an earlier age. Keats believed that the realm of beauty is accessible only at the price of renunciation.[26] Faust cries out:

> What comfort can the shallow world bestow?
> Renunciation!–Learn, man, to forgo!
> This is the lasting theme of themes,
> That soon or late will show its power,
> The tune that lurks in all our dreams,
> And the hoarse whisper of each hour.[27]

The psychic responses to the knowledge that love demands compromise of one's individuality, that literary achievement is accompanied by the trespassing upon one's privacy, and that spiritual immortality requires that one forego *this* life, together constitute the pervasive questing condition about which Emily Dickinson wrote. She believed one cannot steel oneself against anguish and still remain receptive to the affection of others, one cannot withdraw and yet commune, one cannot be both a private poet and a literary celebrity, nor can one embrace the real and ideal at the same time. An undated prose fragment by the poet distills to its essence this theme which is the matrix of the early poetry. She declared: "Consummation is the hurry of fools (exhiliration of fools), but Expectation the Elixir of the Gods."[28] That theme binds into a unity the work of the formative period.

THE QUESTER AND THE QUEEN

Emily Dickinson created in the poetry of her formative years a speaker uniquely appropriate to articulate her theme. In concert with the double aspect of her central concern with the aspiring quest — the emotional throes engendered by the search on the one hand and the triumphant exultation at the visionary apprehension of the goal on the other — the speaker appears both in the role of the humble searcher for fulfillment and the successful explorer who finds imaginatively the treasure of the ideal. One speaks from desire, the other from knowledge. In certain individual poems, the speaker is both persons simultaneously.

In those early works which are informed with a strong sense of personality it is apparent that the world of the speaker is closely circumscribed. The subjects are to a large extent grouped about the central idea of fulfillment. These brief poetic discourses in turn determine the character of the speaker, for it is the situations which that person encounters and her reactions to them that combine to give her a discernible personality. Indeed, because of the relatively small area of experience which the speaker confronts, the focus of the poems returns repeatedly to the interior life of the individual, to the close confines of emotional response, and these responses are often devoid of explicitly narrated causal experiences. In this inner drama, within the diminished stage where the senses register experience and react to it, the speaker is both observer and actor. An analytic view of the inner life exists together with implications of the speaker's emotional investment in what she pictures. Emily Dickinson was aware early in her career of this dual approach in her poems, and was aware, too, that the distinction between objective rendering of experience and subjective infusion of personal feeling was not always to be clearly drawn. The recognition is suggested in the declaration in her first letter to Higginson that her "Mind is so near itself — it cannot see, distinctly" (L–260).

In the occasional friendship pieces, of course, the effectiveness of the feelings rarely ascends beyond conventional expression of sentiment. In other poems, however, which manifest the integrity of the serious artist, the emotion is intense. More important, a growing incisiveness of self-examination, a heuristic process of self-discovery, is represented. The attitudes which are uncovered embody, in turn, a fundamental duality.

This ambivalence of the speaker structures the poem beginning "A Mien to move a Queen" (P–283). At the center of this personality is a divided attitude: on the one hand the person is searcher and sufferer in a world that inflicts pain; on the other hand the person rises victorious over circumstance, becoming the priestess of truths refined from the anguish of experience. The poet's recognition of this contrary orientation reflects the persistent concern in the early poetry with the problem of self-classification. In the early poetry the speaker repeatedly attempts to locate herself in society, in time, and in the moral scale. In effect, the poems ask whether this person, who is compelled to reveal the innermost drama of the emotions, is a barefoot singer or stately queen, lonely lover or wife, playful sprite or saint, martyr of the emotions or poet. Some of these possibilities appear in "A Mien to move a Queen." In the first stanza the character described, like the Maid of Orleans, is both child and heroine:

> A Mien to move a Queen–
> Half Child–Half Heroine–
> An Orleans in the Eye
> That puts it's manner by
> For humbler Company
> When none are near
> Even a Tear–
> It's frequent Visitor.

The contrasting postures of humility and grandeur are expressed succinctly in the opening line. The ambiguous verb "to move" suggests both the humble manner that would impress the sensibility of a queen and the grander manner which allows the speaker to move *as if she were a queen*. The identification of this person with Joan of Arc ("An Orleans in the Eye") argues the strong purposefulness and triumphant manner which mark the personality in other poems. Lines four and five create that opposite, gentler figure who for "humbler Company" becomes humble herself. The closing three lines of the stanza describe the loneliness and private anguish when the regal manner is put by. The same contrasting qualities recur in the second stanza. The royal mien and the noble mind ("A Bonnet like a Duke") exist simultaneously with the shy wren-like manner and the small hands:

> A Bonnet like a Duke–
> And yet a Wren's Peruke
> Were not so shy
> Of Goer by–
> And Hands–so slight–
> They would elate a Sprite
> With Merriment.

The contrary tonalities of this speaker are reasserted in the next stanza. The tone may be soft and enfolding like a snowfall, or it may be as commanding and assured as an empress's:

A Voice that Alters–Low
And on the Ear can go
Like Let of Snow–
Or shift supreme–
As tone of Realm
On Subjects Diadem.

Unable to comprehend such a paradoxical character, other people compromise their disparate reactions and venerate her:

Too small–to fear–
Too distant–to endear–
And so Men Compromise–
And just–revere.

This personality with the contradictory attitudes informs not only many of the early poems, but later ones as well. Consequently, it is a distorting simplification to say, as Archibald MacLeish does, that a single tone controls the poetic expression.[1] Indeed, as the tone changes from the humble to the playful to the imperious, the reader discerns various relationships which this speaker forms with the world of experience. The relationship is as vital to the understanding of certain poems as any other single element. The poet, in effect, like the painter, makes a faithful record not merely of a visual experience but of his whole response to it.[2]

I do not mean to imply that in Emily Dickinson's poetry the speaker's attitudes are limited to the two depicted in "A Mien to move a Queen." At times, indeed, the tone may be burlesque, satirical, or simply narrative. In her first valentine (P–1), for example, the speaker poses as a court judge pronouncing sentence and reveling in his own rhetorical extravagance. The establishment of this playfully pompous relationship to the subject occurs in the lines in which the speaker declares the purpose of the oration:

Now to the *application*, to the reading of the roll,
To bringing thee to justice, and marshalling thy soul.

In another very early poem, " 'Sic transit gloria mundi' " (P–3), similar rhetorical extravagance is apparent; the speaker is a politician, and the tone is gently satirical:

> Unto the Legislature
> My country bids me go;
> I'll take my *india rubbers*,
> In case the *wind* should blow!

In contrast to this lighter, satirical tone, more severe criticism is made in "I've known a Heaven, like a Tent" (P–243). The subject of the declaration in this poem is the disappearance of religious faith. To the denigration of orthodox belief, the idea of heaven is embodied not in such conventional metaphors as light or musical harmony but rather in the metaphor of a traveling circus:

> I've known a Heaven, like a Tent–
> To wrap it's shining Yards–
> Pluck up it's stakes, and disappear–
> Without the sound of Boards
> Or Rip of Nail–Or Carpenter–
> But just the miles of Stare–
> That signalize a Show's Retreat–
> In North America–
>
> No Trace–no Figment of the Thing
> That dazzled, Yesterday,
> No Ring–no Marvel– [3]

Sharp irony also invades the poem "One dignity delays for all" (P–98). To the extent that the attitude in this poem runs directly counter to the consolatory belief that death brings down even the mighty it may be interpreted as a grave criticism of mortal existence. In effect, the speaker is saying that the specious dignity of a funeral awaits even the simple people who in life enjoy no grandeur. The second and fourth stanzas indicate the ironic tone:

> Coach, it insures, and footmen–
> Chamber, and state, and throng–
> Bells, also, in the village
> As we ride grand along!
> . . . .
> How pomp surpassing ermine
> When simple You, and I,
> Present our meek escutscheon
> And claim the rank to die!

In addition, the poem contains sharp irony in the implication of the final line that mortals elect death for its accompanying pageant, though of course in the election they necessarily forego the experience.

Similarly, other early poems reflect an attitude that is neither that of the humble quester nor the queen. These works may for convenience be termed narrative poems. In them the speaker is detached, intent principally on creating a character or situation independent of herself. This dramatizing habit of the poet is apparent even in her letters. The daily affairs of the Dickinson family, for example, are rendered in caricature. In a letter to Mrs. Samuel Bowles, dated by Johnson "about August 1861," the poet writes of her sister and mother: "Vinnie would send her love, but she put on a white frock, and went to meet tomorrow — a few minutes ago. Mother would send her love — but she is in the 'Eave spout,' sweeping up a leaf, that blew in, last November" (L–235). In later correspondence Emily Dickinson often dramatically renders the otherwise homely occurrences in the family. She writes to her cousins about her father's youngest sister Elizabeth: "L[ibbie] goes to Sunderland, Wednesday, for a minute or two; leaves here at 6½ — what a fitting hour — and will breakfast the night before; such a smart atmosphere! The trees stand right up straight when they hear her boots, and will bear crockery wares instead of fruit, I fear. She hasn't starched the geraniums yet, but will have ample time, unless she leaves before April" (L–286, dated 1863). Even the imposing figure of her father did not escape the poet's propensity for caricature: "Father called to say that our steelyard was fraudulent, exceeding by an ounce the rates of honest men. He had been selling oats. I cannot stop smiling, though it is hours since, that even our steelyard will not tell the truth" (L–311, dated 1865).

In comparable manner, Emily Dickinson creates wry dramatic situations in her early poetry. An example is "A little East of Jordan" (P–59):

> A little East of Jordan,
> Evangelists record,
> A Gymnast and an Angel
> Did wrestle long and hard–
>
> Till morning touching mountain–
> And Jacob, waxing strong,
> The Angel begged permission
> To Breakfast–to return–
>
> Not so, said cunning Jacob!
> "I will not let thee go
> Except thou bless me"–Stranger!
> The which acceded to–
>
> Light swung the silver fleeces
> "Peniel" Hills beyond,
> And the bewildered Gymnast
> Found he had worsted God!

In another exercise of her dramatizing ability, Emily Dickinson creates a brief scene in which two lovers overcome their shyness and effect what can only be described as spiritual union (P–208). The artistry, of a low order, is apparent principally in the rhetorical creation of movement through the use of active verbs — "caper," "rose," "fell," "stagger," "fumbled," "danced," and "ticked":

> The Rose did caper on her cheek–
> Her Boddice rose and fell–
> Her pretty speech–like drunken men–
> Did stagger pitiful–

Her fingers fumbled at her work–
Her needle would not go–
What ailed so smart a little Maid–
It puzzled me to know–

Till opposite–I spied a cheek
That bore *another* Rose–
Just opposite–Another speech
That like the Drunkard goes–

A Vest that like her Boddice, danced–
To the immortal tune–
Till those two troubled–little Clocks
Ticked softly into one.

The situation, however trite, is of course an analogue for the poet's central theme of the quest for consummation. The lovers in this drama enact the embarrassment of their separation and the ultimate triumph over it as their hearts merge in "the immortal tune."

Another compact drama is created in "Two swimmers wrestled on the spar" (P–201). The shipwreck metaphor, as we consider it within the thematic matrix outlined in the preceding chapter, suggests that the swimmer who is literally saved by reaching land is also symbolically saved in the religious sense. The other swimmer dies in a gesture of urgent entreaty:

Two swimmers wrestled on the spar–
Until the morning sun–
When One–turned smiling to the land–
Oh God! the Other One!

The stray ships–passing–
Spied a face–
Upon the waters borne–
With eyes in death–still begging raised–
And hands–beseeching–thrown!

The analogue is appropriate to the poet's theme and to the dual aspects of it. One swimmer dies in the anguish of separation, while the other achieves the goal of salvation. Poems in straight narrative are few, however, suggesting that Miss Dickinson knew the most effective treatment of her theme was the lyric, individualized by tone and by the use of novel rhetoric. This individuality enhances the immediacy of the poem as performance. That is, the insistent expression of a particular sensibility makes the person in the poem actively present as speaker. Other devices to create the illusion of spontaneity are analyzed in my later discussion of stylistic techniques.

That orientation of the speaker's attitude that is passive and characterized by humility provides the tonality in a variety of poems. Within them the person is variously searcher, sufferer, meditator on the past and conjuror of the future, and votary in attendance at the ritual of nature. As searcher for consummation, the speaker in "My wheel is in the dark!" (P–10) knows both the loneliness of the quest and the promise of achievement which compels her:

> My foot is on the Tide!
> An unfrequented road–
> Yet have all roads
> A clearing at the end.

The persona in "I never lost as much but twice" (P–49) reveals a curiously compounded attitude of supplication and irreverence as she faces a world given as much to deprivation as to fulfillment. The declaration apparently arises from the speaker's third experience of bereavement:

> I never lost as much but twice,
> And that was in the sod.
> Twice have I stood a beggar
> Before the door of God!
>
> Angels–twice descending
> Reimbursed my store–
> Burglar! Banker–Father!
> I am poor once more!

A supplicatory attitude unqualified by any rebellious turn of mind appears in the elliptic expression in "Jesus! thy Crucifix" (P–225):

> Jesus! thy Crucifix
> Enable thee to guess
> The smaller size!
>
> Jesus! thy second face
> Mind thee in Paradise
> Of our's!

A paraphrase of this austere prayer would read: Jesus! Thy experience of mortality, which ended in the Crucifixion, enables Thee to understand the human predicament. Let the remembrance of that earthly anguish arouse pity in Thee for our present suffering.

The use of the crucifixion metaphor to convey the mortal experience of the speaker who has been denied (or has rejected) earthly honors is present in the middle stanza of "Unto like Story–Trouble has enticed me" (P–295). Here, in addition, the speaker declares her confidence ("I–grown bold") and the strength of her disciplined emotions:

> Unto guessed Crests, my moaning fancy, leads me,
> Worn fair
> By Heads rejected–in the lower country–
> Of honors there–
> Such spirit makes her perpetual mention,
> That I–grown bold–
> Step martial–at my Crucifixion–
> As Trumpets–rolled.

"Guessed Crests," her metaphor of ultimate achievement, is sufficiently ambiguous to encompass the three goals which the poet's persona may be understood to envision: the consummation of desire in love, of poetic labor in posthumous fame, and of spiritual aspiration in immortality. Whatever the goal (or imaginative fusion of goals), the search is pursued with a profound sense of humility combined with intense commitment.

Emily Dickinson's poetic analyses of suffering include a recognition of the consuming nature of pain. Pain, like the panther, can maim its victim with delicate thoroughness (P–244):

> It is easy to work when the soul is at play–
> But when the soul is in pain–
> The hearing him put his playthings up
> Makes work difficult–then–
>
> It is simple, to ache in the Bone, or the Rind–
> But Gimblets–among the nerve–
> Mangle daintier–terribler–
> Like a Panther in the Glove.

Loss may occasion in the speaker a dismay relieved only partially by the pale remembrance of the original joy (P–245):

> I held a Jewel in my fingers–
> And went to sleep–
> The day was warm, and winds were prosy–
> I said "'Twill keep"–
>
> I woke–and chid my honest fingers,
> The Gem was gone–
> And now, an Amethyst remembrance
> Is all I own.

The ambiguous jewel metaphor allows no precise identification of the lost object. One knows only that it was precious and that the remembrance of it is a less precious ("Amethyst") possession. Her use of the word "prosy" to suggest the enervating atmosphere which made the speaker careless of her treasure indicates perhaps that the "jewel" was verbal, a particularly good poetic phrase which could not be recovered after sleep had interrupted composition. Typically, Emily Dickinson creates a recognizable emotion in the poem without any clear reference to the fostering experience. Indeed, the striking expression "Amethyst remembrance" may serve as a touchstone for recognizing other examples of her persistent practice of creating emotion independent of experience, the "spectral power in thought that walks alone," as she wrote to Higginson (L–330) in 1869.

The capacity of the speaker for suffering is infinitely great, as if she could experience the distress of the entire human species (P–264):

> A Weight with Needles on the pounds–
> To push, and pierce, besides–
> That if the Flesh resist the Heft–
> The puncture–cool[l]y tries–
>
> That not a pore be overlooked
> Of all this Compound Frame–
> As manifold for Anguish–
> As Species–be–for name–

This voice belongs to one familiar with distress, who knows that grief is all-engrossing, obliterating sensitive response to any other kind of experience. As noted earlier, the speaker recognizes this in "I felt a Funeral in my Brain." The declaration occurs also in the closing lines of "I got so I could hear his name" (P–293), where misery itself, the speaker says, is "too great, for interrupting — more."

The contrary aspect of this ambivalent voice resounds in poems in which the tone is supremely authoritative, declamatory, omnipotent. An adjunctive gnomic quality intrudes in her letters and accounts for such prose fragments as "Honey grows everywhere but iron (valor) on a Seldom Bush." [4] Both the prose and poetry statements have their provenance in an intense inner strength wrought from crucial experiences. In "I can wade Grief" (P–252), Emily Dickinson employs the metaphor of woven rope to communicate the idea of strength created through deliberate self-control:

> Power is only Pain—
> Stranded, thro' Discipline,
> Till Weights—will hang.

In "Of Bronze—and Blaze" (P–290), the speaker declares her authoritative manner is derived from viewing the magnificence of nature. The aurora borealis, she says:

> Infects my simple spirit
> With Taints of Majesty—
> Till I take vaster attitudes—
> And strut upon my stem—
> Disdaining Men, and Oxygen,
> For Arrogance of them.

In "One Year ago—jots what?" (P–296), the speaker avows an inner strength unsuspected by her lover. She responds to his assertion that his is the more profound sensibility:

> You said it hurt you—most—
> Mine—was an Acorn's Breast—
> And could not know how fondness grew
> In Shaggier Vest—
> Perhaps—I could'nt—
> But, had you looked in—
> A Giant—eye to eye with you, had been—
> No Acorn—then.

The attitude of the speaker as victor over the pain of life, the "pale Reporter, from the awful doors" of death (P–160), is the culminating aspect of this side of the speaker's orientation. She has acquired omniscience out of anguish and perception out of pain. The tone of authority is clear in the opening lines of "I'm 'wife'—I've finished that" (P–199):

> I'm "wife"—I've finished that—
> That other state—
> I'm Czar—I'm "Woman" now—
> It's safer so.

The attitude is clear from the tone of ecstatic assurance in the familiar "I taste a liquor never brewed" (P–214). It reaches one of its most forceful professions in the declaration "Me, change! Me, alter!" (P–268):

> Me, change! Me, alter!
> Then I will, when on the Everlasting Hill
> A Smaller Purple grows–
> At sunset, or a lesser glow
> Flickers upon Cordillera–
> At Day's superior close!

"The poet's soul," John Crowe Ransom says, ". . . must be severe in proportion as the profuse sensibility . . . tends to dissipate and paralyze its force."[5] The frugal economy of the soul is, of course, apparent in this speaker who possesses enormous strength and emotional discipline. These qualities derive from the experiences of anguish, which the speaker confronts. The anguish can repeatedly be related to the condition of separation from the consummate state of mutual love, of poetic achievement, and of spiritual fulfillment. The authoritative qualities derive, indeed, from her triumph over adversity. Emily Dickinson begins a poem of 1862 (P–451) with this quatrain.

> The Outer–from the Inner
> Derives it's Magnitude–
> 'Tis Duke, or Dwarf, according
> As is the Central Mood–

In specific early poems such as "A Mien to move a Queen" and "Of Bronze–and Blaze," both of these qualities of the speaker's character are present. Yet Emily Dickinson's early capabilities are not so confined as this persistent duality suggests, but extended to burlesque, satire, and narrative. The essential duality of her speaker, however, gives us directly and most appropriately the poet's central thematic concern with aspiration. In this quest her speaker both suffers the pain of denial and develops a discipline of the emotions which prevents psychic disintegration. A concomitant of the quest is the visionary achievement of the goal, and in this condition the speaker flaunts her triumphant attitude.

The polarity in both theme and speaker in the early works creates tension which contributes significantly to the effectiveness of the poetry. This effectiveness is artfully enhanced by the poems' characteristic activity as performance, which in turn results from the intimate presence of the speaker. The impact of experience, both real and imagined, on her persona is defined not by the intellect, as in characteristic poetry of the Metaphysicals (with whom Emily Dickinson is somewhat wrongfully compared), but rather by the emotions. Her astonishing control in the early poems over this intense emotional activity is perhaps the most distinguishing mark of her mature artistry in the formative period.

DEVOTIONAL FORM AND
THE CONSTANT OCCASION
FOR IRONY

The attitudes in opposition rendered by Emily Dickinson's poetic voices are by no means the only technical manifestation of the poet's theme of aspiration with its accompanying spectrum of emotions. For operating more subtly at the fundamental level of metrical form are the cadences and connotations of hymnody. The hymn form reinforces with artfully subdued persuasion the aspiring quest for consummation. The form also provides for an ingenious complexity arising from a persistent secularity of attitude and language in counterpoint to the devotional schema. Hymnody, that is, provides a constant occasion for irony.

Emily Dickinson's hymn forms are not invariably the controlling frames, however. In the early years a significant part of her creative energies was devoted to experimentation, sometimes within the hymn form and sometimes so unfettered as to constitute *vers libre*. On a few occasions she allowed the poetic impulse to create its own most immediate, if somewhat formless, expression. But by far the greatest number of her early poems she composed within the constraints of the relatively few and most common hymn forms. Whether one calls her recurrent four-stress-three-stress pattern the "fourteener," the "ballad meter" or the "common meter" of hymnody depends somewhat upon where in the historical evolution of English prosody one chooses his terms. A clarification of terminology will be useful.

The "fourteener" line of seven iambic feet, a popular form in the thirteenth century, split at a later date, according to George Saintsbury, into what is commonly called the ballad measure.[1] The seven iambics, a form determined by both the accentual count and the syllabic count, became separated into four iambics or eight syllables, with the remaining three iambics forming the second line of six syllables. The syllabic pattern eight-six-eight-six resulted. In this ballad measure of alternating octosyllables and hexasyllables the even lines always rhyme and the odd lines rhyme "not uncommonly."[2] From this ballad quatrain, evidently, evolved the hymn form known as "common measure." Saintsbury distinguishes between the hymn and ballad forms by asserting that common measure is usually restricted to eights and sixes without substitution; that is, the hymn meter tends to be more regular than the ballad. A more fundamental distinction exists, however, and must be recognized in a discussion of Emily Dickinson's poetry, for she clearly felt free to make extensive substitution in the metrical patterns. The essential distinction between the ballad and the hymn resides in both the content and the treatment. The ballad genre most often combines the narrative and lyric modes, while in the hymn the narrative intent is rare.[3] Like the hymn, Emily Dickinson's verse employs for unique purposes the devotional tone associated with that genre. The hymn is the controlled, formalized expression of the intense impulses of aspiration and devotion. Isaac Watts (1674–1748) describes these tonal characteristics in his preface to *Hymns and Spiritual Songs* (London, 1709), where he urges the exorcism of "Evil Expressions" from religious songs: "It comes to pass, that when spiritual Affections are excited within us, and our Souls are raised a little above this Earth in the beginning of a Psalm, we are check'd on a sudden in our Ascent toward Heaven by some Expressions that are more suited to the Days of *Carnal Ordinances*, and fit only to be sung in the *Worldly Santuary*."[4] These qualities of spiritual elevation one does not normally associate with the ballad. Indeed, we will discover that Emily Dickinson manipulated with wit and ironic effect the tonal connotations of the hymn.

The "short measure" of the hymn books seems, according to Saintsbury, to have evolved from the poulter's measure. This derivation explains Yvor Winters' use of the latter term to identify a persistent formal arrangement in Emily Dickinson's poetry.[5] Short meter derives from the combination of the alexandrine line and the fourteener, that is, from a line of twelve syllables (or six iambics) followed by a line of fourteen syllables (or seven iambics). Saintsbury concludes that the alexandrine was broken up into two lines of six syllables and the fourteener into a line of eight and a line of six.[6] One finds evolved, then, the short-measure syllabic pattern of six-six-eight-six. The "long measure" of the hymn books is a variation of common meter: each line is eight syllables. The most common hymn forms, then, are common meter (alternating eight and six syllables to the line), long meter (eight syllables to the line), and short meter (two lines of six syllables, followed by one of eight, and then one of six).[7]

The stanzaic arrangement of these meters is normally four lines but each can be extended to six or to eight lines. In extension, they become "common particular meter," with the syllabic count of eight-eight-six-eight-eight-six, and "short particular meter," with the syllabic count of six-six-eight-six-six-eight. Other common arrangements are "sevens and sixes," where the common meter drops the final accented syllable in the longer lines, leaving an alternating syllabic count but organizing the stresses into a regular pattern of three beats. Regular lines of sixes also form a common pattern of hymnody. Though usually iambic in movement, these latter two forms, the "sevens and sixes" and "sixes," lend themselves also to a trochaic rhythm. Emily Dickinson, in a few poems and in particular lines within an otherwise generally iambic pattern, employs these meters for a trochaic movement.

The principal trochaic meters in the hymn books are "sevens," "eights and sevens," "eights and fives," "sevens and fives," "sixes and fives," and "sixes." Although Johnson asserts in his critical biography that "every poem [Emily Dickinson] composed before 1861 . . . is fashioned in one or another of [the] hymn meters," the fact is that more than fifty of the poems in those early years have thoroughly mixed meters and display only a remote connection to regular hymn meters, the relationship apparent chiefly in the reliance on lines of four stresses or fewer.[8]

That Isaac Watts was the principal transmitter of the verse forms which Emily Dickinson uses seems indisputable. The evidence, however, is largely circumstantial. Her father had in his library editions of Watts's *Christian Psalmody* and *The Psalms, Hymns, and Spiritual Songs*.[9] The general popularity of Watts at the time is indicated by Timothy Dwight's "Advertisement" in his edition of psalms and hymns: "The reverence for Doctor *Watts* is in this country so great that I shall not be surprised to find myself charged with want of modesty for suggesting that he was the subject of . . . errors [in language and sentiment]."[10] Dwight's edition was itself the most popular collection of Watts in the early nineteenth century, according to Henry W. Foote in his standard study of American hymnody:

> In the first quarter of the century, indeed down to about 1840, the book most widely used among the more conservative Congregationalists and the Presbyterians was the one . . . which had been edited by Timothy Dwight, and was commonly called *Dwight's Watts*. In 1815 appeared another book which, in its revised form, was destined to be a rival of Dwight's in orthodox Congregational circles. It was prepared by Rev. Samuel Worcester of Salem, Massachusetts, and was called *Christian Psalmody, in four parts: Comprising Dr. Watts' Psalms abridged: Select Hymns from other sources; and select Harmonies*. It was an excellent selection, the fourth part consisting of eighty-two good tunes at the back of the book. Unfortunately, Worcester had underestimated the attachment of the churches to Watts, for he had made room for new hymns by grouping some of Watts' psalms, and shortening others. Immediately a clamor arose

against "mangling" and "amputating" and "robbing" Watts, and a demand for "Watts entire." So, against his better judgment, Worcester brought out in 1819 a second and inferior book which contained the complete *Psalms and Hymns* by Watts, with other selected hymns, but without music. This book, entitled *The Psalms, Hymns and Spiritual Songs of the Reverend Isaac Watts, to which are added Select Hymns from other authors*, but commonly called *Watts and Select*, had a lasting vogue, especially in the churches which were inclined to dispute the right of any other authors to trespass on the sacred field where Watts now reigned supreme.[11]

Emily Dickinson's early experience of Watts's hymns can be inferred from the impression they made upon her brother Austin:

In Emily's childhood, hymns (Watts's hymns in particular) were sung in church, but without accompaniment until an innovation was introduced when her brother was about ten. To the end of his life Austin Dickinson recalled the impression it made upon him: "In 1839 . . . came the acquisition of the first musical instrument ever owned by the parish, a double bass viol. With my first recollection Josiah Ayres managed it, and the tones he drew from its lower chords in his accompaniment to the singing of some of Watts's Favorite Hymns, haunt me even now. Such lines as
'That awful day will surely come,'
'That last great day of woe and doom,'
and
'Broad is the road that leads to death,' etc.
seemed to me sufficiently depressing in plain print; sung with the accompaniment they were appalling — to a boy."[12]

There is no explicit reference to Isaac Watts in Emily Dickinson's letters. Two lines in a poem dated 1859 (P–112), however, clearly echo lines in Watts's hymn beginning "There is a land of pure delight."[13] The lines which open the last stanza in Watts read:

Could we but climb where Moses stood,
And view the landscape o'er.

The first two lines of the last stanza of Emily Dickinson's poem are enclosed in quotation marks:

> "Oh could we climb where Moses stood,
> And view the Landscape o'er."

The tone of Emily Dickinson's poem is a curious overlay of whimsy upon the more serious search for the bliss of heaven. The first two stanzas reflect the mixed tone by ambiguously referring to "Pater," who may be interpreted either as God or as the poet's father:

> Where bells no more affright the morn–
> Where scrabble never comes–
> Where very nimble Gentlemen
> Are forced to keep their rooms–
>
> Where tired Children placid sleep
> Thro' Centuries of noon
> This place is Bliss–this town is Heaven–
> Please, Pater, pretty soon!

The final stanza, however, concludes:

> Not Father's bells–nor Factories,
> Could scare us any more!

These lines return one to Amherst from the vision of a heavenly nursery where children sleep "thro' Centuries of noon." Emily Dickinson employs in the beginning the devout tone of the hymn but almost immediately counterpoints, by her choice of diction, a secular whimsicality. Where Watts sings of the land of pure delight "Where saints immortal reign," Emily Dickinson writes of the place "Where very nimble Gentlemen/ Are forced to keep their rooms." Not only does she by the homely language and whimsical situation establish the playful quality of the fervor of her plea (that she be allowed to sleep later in the mornings); she has injected the heretical notion that the repose of interment (the confining "rooms") might be more desired than paradisiacal transport. Further on we will follow her more intricate use of the tonal connotations of the hymn. For now we must recognize that Emily Dickinson was familiar with Watts. Moreover, her persistent use of the hymn form is evidence that when she mused upon her theme, whether in whimsical or devout mood (or in a mood constituted of both), the rhythm of the articulating voice within her moved in the meter and in the line length and syntactical concision of the hymn. Through it she refracted the special light of her own beliefs.

Of the three hundred poems presumably from this period, well over two thirds (233 poems) are regularly iambic or have an iambic base. Of this portion one hundred thirty-three (almost half of her total output to 1862) follow a regular metrical movement with little significant variation.[14] These more obvious formal impositions, however, should not obscure her reliance upon hymnal *tone* and *language*. These elements contribute in significant measure to the textural density of Emily Dickinson's poetry. The following illustrations from Watts and Dickinson are not intended to trace a line of descent from the hymns; the purpose rather is to show her use of the hymn schema *as poetic device* and to reveal its contribution to the complex manner of the poet's method.

Hymn Forty-One of Watts's collection is appropriate as illustration for it exhibits regular common meter, employs some of Watts's recurrent imagery, and embodies clearly the devotional tone that informs the genre.[15]

> These glorious minds, how bright they shine!
>   Whence all their white array?
> How came they to the happy seats
>   Of everlasting day?
>
> From tort'ring pains to endless joys,
>   On fiery wheels they rode;
> And strangely wash'd their raiments white,
>   In Jesus' dying blood.
>
> Now they approach a spotless God,
>   And bow before his throne;
> Their warbling harps, and sacred songs
>   Adore the Holy One.

The unveil'd glories of his face
　　Amongst his saints reside;
While the rich treasures of his grace
　　See all their wants supplied.

Tormenting thirst shall leave their souls,
　　And hunger flee as fast;
The fruit of life's immortal tree
　　Shall be their sweet repast.

The Lamb shall lead his heavenly flock,
　　Where living fountains rise;
And love divine shall wipe away
　　The sorrows of their eyes.

The tone here, deliberate and devotional, rises from the opening question which asks how the blessed arrive at the divine state. The declaration follows that through purification by anguish, their own upon earth and Christ's upon the cross, they have been elevated above the condition of relief to a final state of ecstatic freedom from anguish. In the hymn book, in fact, the song is marked to be sung in "soft tones," then "slow and loud," then "loud." The song is a lyric of exultation and affirmation of faith. It is an expression of faith in the ultimate cessation of anguish and in fulfillment through divine love. The figurative language, certainly not unique with Watts, includes images and ideas repeatedly found in Emily Dickinson's poetry: the depiction of the heavenly state as "everlasting day," the transition from earthly anguish to heavenly relief and repose, the hierarchical organization of the heavenly hosts, the imaging of bliss as a treasure store, and the use of the analogies of thirst and hunger for the unfulfilled aspiration of the soul. The contrasting states of aspiration and consummation are conditions also depicted repeatedly in Emily Dickinson's poetry.

The movement toward affirmation of the divine goal, in an identical pattern of deliberation rising to a final pitch of exultation, appears, for example, in "She bore it till the simple veins"

(P–144). The same concept of compensation for a life of anguish underlies this poem:

> She bore it till the simple veins
> Traced azure on her hand–
> Till pleading, round her quiet eyes
> The purple Crayons stand.
>
> Till Daffodils had come and gone
> I cannot tell the sum,
> And then she ceased to bear it–
> And with the Saints sat down.
>
> No more her patient figure
> At twilight soft to meet–
> No more her timid bonnet
> Upon the village street–
>
> But Crowns instead, and Courtiers–
> And in the midst so fair,
> Whose but her shy–immortal face
> Of whom we're whispering here?

Though the tone in many respects is similar, Emily Dickinson has attempted to individualize the situation. She describes a single person in the homely yet vivid imagery of pain's physical marks. This mode of particularizing is characteristic of Emily Dickinson; in her finest poetry it is the device which provides immediacy and relevance, transforming the abstract and metaphysical into the concrete. The metrical base of this poem is common meter, but the poet has altered the pattern in the middle two stanzas, dropping from three of the normally octosyllabic lines the final stressed syllable. The effect is to suggest a tentative state still to be resolved. The final affirmation of the heavenly state, however, moves in the more deliberate and more regularly accented common measure. The underlying metrical pattern provides the base for this effective manipulation of rhythm. The tonal connotation of the hymn form reinforces the movement toward the final declaration of achievement of immortality.

Common meter (not surprisingly) also served Emily Dickinson in her occasional friendship notes where the sentiment is subdued and the declaration of affection more or less conventional, as in "My Eye is fuller than my vase" (P–202):

> My Eye is fuller than my vase–
> *Her* Cargo–is of Dew–
> And still–my Heart–my Eye outweighs–
> East India–for you!

In this verse, where little freedom in diction or rhythm is taken, the common meter reverts to its rocking movement, creating a facetiousness as much dependent on the obtrusive rhyme as upon the triteness of the sentiment and language. Many of Emily Dickinson's poems descend to this level of the casual and the obvious, to the *compromised* poetic impulse which exposes the weakness of the hymn meter. In such pieces she relaxed her powers of insight and composition, letting the meter carry the burden, rather than working subtly upon the meter itself to create complexity. In poems such as this, the metrical inadequacies of hymnody are revealed.

An early poem which demonstrates the effects Emily Dickinson could contrive out of the common meter is "Going to Heaven!" (P–79). She takes as deliberate liberties with the metrical form as she does with the devotional tone. The line arrangement does not follow the typically regular disposition of lines in the hymn pattern, yet in reading the poem, one recognizes the underlying regularity of the four-three stress arrangement (as in common meter). This even measure, in turn, is reinforced by a *general* adherence to the syllabic count which characterizes hymn verses. And reinforcing both the stress and syllabic patterns, the rhyme scheme, with two exceptions, serves to structure the lines

in a way similar to the hymn. The first stanza affords examples
of the use of these three elements of line, stress, and rhyme
pattern:

> Going to Heaven!
> I don't know when–
> Pray do not ask me how!
> Indeed I'm too astonished
> To think of answering you!
> Going to Heaven!
> How dim it sounds!
> And yet it will be done
> As sure as flocks go home at night
> Unto the Shepherd's arm!

The rhyme scheme patterns the first five lines. Lines three and
five end in a vowel rhyme. A closer analysis of this particular
device, recurrent in Emily Dickinson's poetry, reveals that the
vowel rhyme pairs a simple vowel with a diphthong: the ending
in both *you* and *how* is the "u" sound. The rhyme makes an
auditory line arrangement somewhat different from the actual
line disposition. We now recognize that lines one and two taken
together form an octosyllabic unit with four stresses. The pattern
which emerges has as its base the common meter lines of eight
and six syllables. In the first stanza, one discovers the syllabic
pattern to be eight (four plus four), six, eight, six, eight (four
plus four), six, eight, six. The stresses, when the lines are ordered
according to the rhyme pattern, are regular four-three, including
line four in which the final syllable is accented. Greater freedom
with both the stress and syllabic counts is apparent in the remaining two stanzas; yet the recurrence in alternate lines of the
regular six-syllable, three-stress pattern establishes the common
meter movement. The disposition of the other lines into seven,
eight, and nine syllables and generally four-stress movements
sustains the base pattern of the common meter:

Perhaps you're going too!
Who knows?
If you sh'd get there first
Save just a little place for me
Close to the two I lost–
The smallest "Robe" will fit me
And just a bit of "Crown"–
For you know we do not mind our dress
When we are going home–

I'm glad I dont believe it
For it w'd stop my breath–
And I'd like to look a little more
At such a curious Earth!
I am glad they did believe it
Whom I have never found
Since the mighty Autumn afternoon
I left them in the ground.

This freedom in the employment of the common meter is not so great that the discipline is lost, yet the freedom allows the informality of direct address. Metrical variations provide an effective disconcertion of the reader's expectations. This technique creates rhythmically a tension and an engagement; that is, one's effort to perceive the swing of a regular pattern is almost continually thwarted, and yet the suggestion of regularity is strong enough to evoke this continual effort. And of course the rhythmic disconcertion reinforces the content of the poem. For the attitude, contrary to the hymnal tone of devotion, shifts abruptly from breathless awe at the thought of heaven to a declaration of skepticism:

I'm glad I dont believe it
For it w'd stop my breath.

The final lines close in a paradoxical mixture of awe at the fact of death and recognition of the pragmatic value of faith. The wayward verse form, then, is perfectly appropriate to the tonal liberties which counterpoint the speaker's skepticism against the sustaining faith possessed by the "two I lost."

Other liberties in the poem also disconcert the reader who anticipates the conventional feeling that the underlying hymn design promises. The breathlessness of the first stanza, for example, is a *personal* reaction to the thought of death and immortality, and not the ceremonious avowal of faith and humility:

> Pray do not ask me how!
> Indeed I'm too astonished
> To think of answering you!

This active presence of the speaker is effected by conversational language, creating again a counterpoint of the homely and the colloquial to the exalted subject and to the devotional connotation of the hymn form. The breathlessness is interrupted momentarily by the orthodox doctrinal assertion:

> And yet it will be done
> As sure as flocks go home at night
> Unto the Shepherd's arm!

The beginning of the second stanza departs again from anticipated orthodoxy, returning to the conversational and the closely personal. The imagery is typical of Emily Dickinson when she descends to materializing the eternal in the objects of girlhood. But as the poem moves into the final stanza it surprises us by the bold, clear assertion of a dominant secular interest:

> I'm glad I don't believe it
> For it w'd stop my breath.

The rebellious pilgrim, disavowing a faith in the eternal life, makes an assertion in direct contrast to the assurance one finds in the line "And yet it will be done." We see here that fundamental division in the speaker's mind which is reflected in the more subtle counterpoint that has been created all along through diction and metrical variations. The ambiguity in these two lines reinforces the dilemma of faith already established. The rejection of faith is reasoned in the next two lines in the assertion that this earth offers too much, at least for the present, to be rejected. At this crucial point in the poem the speaker recognizes that aspiration may exist *without* faith.

The disjunction is central to Emily Dickinson's attitude in the early poems and it underlies her unique use of the hymn verse patterns. One may aspire to the ideal, to complete and eternal fulfillment, and one may employ conventional devices of meter and devotional diction to convey this impulse of aspiration, but the attitude may exist separate from orthodox belief in immortality. Emily Dickinson has used the form for more than simply a metrical vehicle.[16] She has made it intrinsically functional as it contributes to the fundamental tension and ambivalence. The incongruity of form and content provides the metrical correlative of the unconventionality of the belief. In more whimsical form, this incongruity may operate as parody; in its more serious intent it is effective irony, and in its ultimate form, as both idea and art, it is an act of profound insight into the personal dilemma of faith. At each dimension, from the metrical representation to the philosophical level, the dialectic operates. The poetry, in the end, re-enacts a testing of received faith by the experience of the actual. This confrontation explains why her best and, I should say, her typical, poems begin in innocence and end in fright, take their direction in desire and terminate in doubt.

Of the iambic verse Emily Dickinson wrote, about a fourth has no discernible tie to hymnody. Composed in short lines ranging from one to four stresses, these irregular verses seem to have acquired their formal arrangement from strong psychological pressures. The influence of the concision and metrical limitations of the hymn is clear, but one is not made aware of the tonal connotations of the hymn. It is significant, for example, that in the poem "I'm 'wife'—I've finished that" (P–199), where the attitude is not one of aspiration but rather of achievement at having reached a state of fulfillment, neither the common meter nor the other principal hymn meters are used. The profound reaction to the experience of maturation seems to dictate the metrical pattern. In the opening stanza (disregarding for the moment the poet's own line arrangement), we find a rare instance of iambic pentameter:

> I'm "wife"–I've finished that–
> That other state–
> I'm Czar–I'm "Woman" now–
> It's safer so.

The quiet firmness contrasts with the breathless tone of many of the other poems. The short lines are perfectly appropriate to the emotional vibrancy of the situation. The speaker's declarations, impulsive and intense, lend themselves to expression in the unusually clipped line and the limited stress pattern. The first stanza declares the condition of the speaker, announcing that a profound transition has taken place which is not simply from girlhood to womanhood, for the poet has enclosed the words *wife* and *woman* in quotation marks, a device to remove the normal denotations. The second stanza elaborates, through the perception of hindsight, on the immensity of the change. The quality of the change progresses from being simply "odd" to being apocalyptic. The nature of the new commitment which the speaker feels is not specified, but rather is the sort of unnamed commitment, the appropriation of an obligation that somehow changes one's life, to which she alludes in other poems:

> How odd the Girl's life looks
> Behind this soft Eclipse–
> I think that Earth feels so
> To folks in Heaven–now–
>
> This being comfort–then
> That other kind–was pain–
> But why compare?
> I'm "Wife"! Stop there!

It is unnecessary to speculate whether in fact Emily Dickinson here means a commitment to a lover, for example, or a personal commitment to the poetic life. Her important discovery is that she is able to comprehend a profound transformation into maturity. The finality of the declaration is locked tightly in the short lines and terminal accents.

Of particular interest in a study of her metrics are the poems in which she abandons altogether the regular metrical forms. Such poems do not constitute a considerable part of her early work or even of the total body of work, but they are important in demonstrating the freedom with which she experiments and the reaches of her early talent. The results range from the merely indicative to achievements of a high quality. In "Ah, Moon–and Star!" (P–240), for example, though some genuine feeling seems latent, the composition never rises to eloquence. The poem represents perhaps more clearly than any other from the early years the decline of some of her verse into the baroque prose one finds in her letters. The opening two lines are embarrassingly uninspired, and those that follow defy satisfactory scansion:

> Ah, Moon–and Star!
> You are very far–
> But were no one
> Farther than you–
> Do you think I'd stop
> For a Firmament–
> Or a Cubit–or so?

Other experimentations were more successful. Perhaps the most interesting is "Wild Nights–Wild Nights!" (P–249). One might in that poem, relying on the rhyme pattern, reassemble the lines into "eights" in the first stanza, "nines" in the second, and "eights" again in the third stanza. The strength of the exclamation, however, would seem to prohibit longer lines which would deny the utter exultation, for example, of the visionary climax "Ah, the Sea!" The clipped lines and the general pattern of two stresses render perfectly the tone of fervent pleading and aspiration. The poem embodies the characteristically divided view noted earlier in "Going to Heaven!" (P–79). Here the emotional counterpoint is between the attraction of an ideal repose and the turmoil of a strong emotional commitment; it is the heart's plea for fulfillment even at the price of spiritual salvation. The dialectic controls the movement of the poem. The first stanza expresses a clear and powerful impulse for union, to the making of unity out of twain:

> Wild Nights–Wild Nights!
> Were I with thee
> Wild Nights should be
> Our luxury!

The next lines reflect from the speaker's mind the possibilities of another state, that of Eden and of the calm at the end of the quest. As if to show the persuasiveness of this other vision, she extends the thought one line into the third stanza:

> Futile–the Winds–
> To a Heart in port–
> Done with the Compass–
> Done with the Chart!
>
> Rowing in Eden.

This conjectured calm is specious, however, for while it may promise both the security and repose of immortality, it involves also the futility of a state where the most profound experiences are impossible. In resolution, she opts for the dangerous course:

> Ah, the Sea!
> Might I but moor–Tonight–
> In Thee!

The sea is one of Emily Dickinson's diffuse symbols. In "Wild Nights–Wild Nights!" it may represent both lover and immortality. It is perhaps best interpreted as a fusion of the two in which there is an undefined convergence of earthly and divine love. Because of the erotic connotations the poem has evoked wide comment. But for the present purpose it is enough to note how the poem's surging vitality breaks out of the poet's characteristic restraint within the regular or near-regular line patterns of the hymn book. If the hymn form was yet a major influence in Emily Dickinson's stylistic development toward extreme concision in expression, it was, in fact, not concise enough when the impulse was so intense it defied elaboration.

Obviously Emily Dickinson developed remarkably as an artist in the early years. The evidence is clear when one compares her first valentine to this poem which addresses itself to the same theme. The greater concision is first apparent, but the artistic maturation is indicated by the fact that the more concise of the two works is the more complex, suggesting as it does the tragic emotional dilemma issuing in the deliberate choice of the more difficult course. The possibilities of interpretation radiate from this brief poem. As in so many of Emily Dickinson's works, it is the *emotion* which emerges intense and precise, while the circumstances of the emotion remain dissociated. The quest for immortality can equally well be understood as the quest for an earthly union. She gives us not the exact definition of a *situation* but the intense moment of feeling, flashing independent, as she says in a later poem (P–365), from its creative source.

> Least Village has it's Blacksmith
> Whose Anvil's even ring
> Stands symbol for the finer Forge
> That soundless tugs–within–
> Refining these impatient Ores
> With Hammer, and with Blaze
> Until the Designated Light
> Repudiate the Forge–

One may with assurance make three emphatic assertions concerning the verse forms which Emily Dickinson employed in the early years. In poems which depart from hymnody, one finds the meter-making impulse that is apparent in "Wild Nights–Wild Nights!" But Emily Dickinson learned her craft from the hymn books, and working with the brief lines of the devotional hymn she recreated both a more intense and a more private attitude of aspiration. Perhaps this clipped form reflects the laconic speech of the New England Yankee, careful of his words, his emotions in tight control. But the fact of art is that Emily Dickinson clipped her poetic expression because the sharp emotional pang is faithfully conveyed in the concisest form, and because that technique stands symbol for the spirit's austerity in the presence of emotional upheaval.

Secondly, the poet's use of the hymn form as the *discipline* upon which she worked her variations is inseparable from the act of aspiration which constitutes her central theme. The form embodies her teleological emphasis. This is not to insist that Emily Dickinson employed the form consciously. It would be more valid, perhaps, to say that this cadence came to frame her thoughts prior to her need to articulate the feelings she experienced. As her range of insight developed and as she was able more precisely to comprehend the inner drama of anguish and aspiration she recreated the experience in the metrical framework already possessed. She necessarily viewed her theme of aspiration through that rhythmic medium; what she experienced of the inmost life she perceived through the *possibilities* of her metrics. She did not confront her theme with a large variety of possible verse forms in which to express it. Rather, she engaged her theme with the limited formal habits of the hymn, and the hymn form determined ultimately *what she saw*. It became for her *her mode of perception*, the metrical schema which she modified as the necessity of her impulse dictated. As Mr. Blackmur has said of the relationship between poetic form and experience, the poetry "organizes the content of the world as it passes before the poet, but the forms in which that content is organized come out of the structure of poetry itself." [17]

Finally, in the early poems which are in regular or nearly regular verse patterns like common meter, the hymn form as employed by Emily Dickinson provides a *constant occasion for irony*. Inherent in the hymn form is the attitude of faith, humility, and aspiration, and it is against this base of orthodoxy that she so artfully refracts the personal rebellion and individual feeling, the colloquial diction and syntax, the homely image, the scandalous love of this world, and the habitual religious skepticism. In its least effective form this counterpoint creates mere playfulness. But when the counterpoint succeeds, the use of the occasion for irony makes possible an intensity and tonal friction of strictest concision. In a purely technical regard, the hymn schema performs a function absolutely appropriate to the impulse of this poet. A measure of her early artistry is the richness and density of effect she achieved by working out from that apparently simple and constraining formal base.

MOTION, REST, AND
METAMORPHOSIS

No single characteristic of Emily Dickinson's early poetry is more prominent than its representation of movement. Her kinesthetic imagery by its persistence constitutes the central visual metaphor by which she apprehends experience. She confronts repeatedly the inescapable riddle of physical and spiritual change, movement, and metamorphosis, and this concern mirrors directly the polar disposition of the real and the conjectured, the actual and the ideal, which engaged her attention. Movement and change represent for Emily Dickinson the process by which one passes from personal isolation to a consummate union, from artistic endeavor to literary immortality, and from spiritual aspiration to spiritual immortality. In more abstract terms, the process is the change from the condition of possibility — emotional, artistic, spiritual — to the state of self-fulfillment, "Existence's whole Arc filled up," as she says in a later poem (P–508).

The inhering unity of the early poetry is formed in part by the recurrent kinetic imagery, as unity derives also from the controlling theme, the characteristic duality of the persona, and formal base of hymnody. The creative artistry, in turn, is manifested in the individual manner with which Emily Dickinson employs her images, and particularly in the way they objectify both the tension of emotional turmoil and the perceived flux in the outer world of nature. In "An altered look about the hills" (P–140), the depiction of motion dramatizes the irrevocable yet almost imperceptible onset of spring:

An altered look about the hills–
A Tyrian light the village fills–
A wider sunrise in the morn–
A deeper twilight on the lawn–
A print of a vermillion foot–
A purple finger on the slope–
A flippant fly upon the pane–
A spider at his trade again–
An added strut in Chanticleer–
A flower expected everywhere–
An axe shrill singing in the woods–
Fern odors on untravelled roads–
All this and more I cannot tell–
A furtive look you know as well–
And Nicodemus' Mystery
Receives it's annual reply!

The allusion "Nicodemus' Mystery" in line fifteen refers to the Biblical passage John 3.4, in which Nicodemus asks Christ how rebirth is possible: "Nicodemus said to him, 'How can a man be born when he is old? Can he enter a second time into his mother's womb and be born?'" In Emily Dickinson's typology, spring symbolizes the resurrection. Nature's awakening is the annual metamorphosis, audible and visible, and the natural correlative of Christ's reply to Nicodemus: "Do not marvel that I said to you, 'You must be born anew.'" In the poem the verbs denote action and sound and are adroitly reinforced by adjectives of change and motion — *altered, wider, deeper, added,* and *furtive.*

The range of intensity of movement which Emily Dickinson creates extends far beyond the examples in this early treatment of nature's subtle alterations. Perhaps her ultimate expression is in the late poem "A Route of Evanescence" (P–1463), which can serve here as a touchstone for her kinetic imagery in the earlier works. The imagery is of whirring, scarcely visible, flight:

A Route of Evanescence
With a revolving Wheel–
A Resonance of Emerald–
A Rush of Cochineal–
And every Blossom on the Bush
Adjusts it's tumbled Head–
The mail from Tunis, probably,
An easy Morning's Ride–

The poet's maturing facility of expression is apparent in the contrasting treatments in the two poems. In "An altered look about the hills" she suggests movement by the auditory and visual connotations of the verbs and adjectives; in this later poem (dated 1879 by Johnson) there are but three kinesthetic adjectives — *revolving, tumbled, easy* — and only a single verb — *adjusts*. The vivid auditory representation of the hummingbird's motion is achieved by alliteration — *Route, revolving, Resonance, Rush* — as well as by consonance — *Evanescence, Resonance, Blossom, Adjusts, Tunis, Rush, Bush, easy* and *Morning's*. The words, significantly, which evoke the sense of motion are, with few exceptions, nouns. In effect, the pressure of motion is so intense it has imbued normally inert abstractions with the illusion of speed so rapid, as in the flight of the hummingbird, that the eye is less useful than the ear, and the ear less perceptive than the imagination. The bird darts so quickly only the sound lingers and to the eye only the tumbled blossoms give evidence of the flight.

In contrast to the intention in this remarkable poem is the imagery in another familiar work which can serve as a touchstone for the poet's creation of absolute stasis. In "After great pain, a formal feeling comes" (P–341), the condition is not one of motion, but of the inertia which grief brings on. Again, nouns do the most effective metaphorical work. *Tombs, stone, lead,* and *snow* provide visual and tactile immediacy to the condition of paralysis induced by grief:

After great pain, a formal feeling comes–
The Nerves sit ceremonious, like Tombs–
The stiff Heart questions was it He, that bore,
And Yesterday, or Centuries before?

The Feet, mechanical, go round–
Of Ground, or Air, or Ought–
A Wooden way
Regardless grown,
A Quartz contentment, like a stone–

This is the Hour of Lead–
Remembered, if outlived,
As Freezing persons, recollect the Snow–
First–Chill–then Stupor–then the letting go.

Her reliance on motion and stasis as perceptive frames for her poetry has attracted little critical comment. Richard Chase's insight is the most noteworthy: "At the heart of Emily Dickinson's vision of death . . . is the sensation of motion and rest. Almost any persistent motion, almost any condition of stasis, in nature or human existence, was likely to summon up in her mind this beautiful and menacing power."[1] Yet suggestive as the assertion is, it constricts any attempt to define the meanings Emily Dickinson attaches to motion and to the absence of motion. In the hummingbird poem quoted above, for example, she delights in picturing motion for its own sake, without any rooted concern with death. In the early poem "I counted till they danced so" (P–36), she pictures dancing snowflakes, and the image she creates has no further extension as a symbol of death.

I counted till they danced so
Their slippers leaped the town,
And then I took a pencil
To note the rebels down.
And then they grew so jolly
I did resign the prig,
And ten of my once stately toes
Are marshalled for a jig!

She does in other early poems, to be sure, make the identification between snow and the cold fearful silence of death. In "The only Ghost I ever saw" (P–274), the first stanza draws the equation with the "Ghost":

> The only Ghost I ever saw
> Was dressed in Mechlin–so–
> He had no sandal on his foot–
> And stepped like flakes of snow.

The final stanza represents the speaker's reflection on the thought of death evoked by her experience of a snow storm:

> Our interview–was transient–
> Of me, himself was shy–
> And God forbid I look behind–
> Since that appalling Day!

The much-anthologized early poem "She sweeps with many-colored Brooms" (P–219) is representative also of poems from the early group in which the shifting motions of the organic world merely delight rather than signify. The evening wind works through the trees ("her spotted brooms"), scattering the autumn leaves. The observer lifts her head skyward as the wind subsides (the "Brooms fade softly into stars"), and then, lowering her gaze, she walks away:

> And still, she plies her spotted Brooms,
> And still the Aprons fly,
> Till Brooms fade softly into stars–
> And then I come away.

Chase's assertion, besides being too restrictive, neglects the *qualitative* meanings that attach to Emily Dickinson's concern with motion. Not only do motion and stasis suggest to her life and death, but they also imply respectively the conditions of aspiration and achievement, of shifting doubt stabilizing into inflexible faith, of resurrection terminating in the ultimate haven of immortality, of the activity of earthly existence passing in death to the motionless retirement within the tomb, and of the poetic labors producing the enduring artifact of poetry. In her recurrent acknowledgment of flux she is closest in vision to the American Transcendentalists, yet the similarity provides only limited usefulness. For the Transcendental vision is circular and solipsistic. In Emily Dickinson's vision the flux presses irrevocably along a single temporal plane, creating change and absolute disjunction. Very early in her career she had with analytic clarity defined for herself this central perception:

> Some things that fly there be–
> Birds–Hours–the Bumblebee–
> Of these no Elegy.
>
> Some things that stay there be–
> Grief–Hills–Eternity–
> Nor this behooveth me.
>
> There are that resting, rise.
> Can I expound the skies?
> How still the Riddle lies!   (P–89)

The three stanzas represent distinctly and concisely the thematic locus defined earlier. In order, they catalogue types of the *actual*, the *ideal*, and the process of *metamorphosis* which carries from the actual to the ideal. It is the final riddle of the incompossible achieved that constitutes the heart of the theme to which she constantly addressed herself. Typically in this poem the riddle of metamorphosis (in other poems, the seed in the ground that blooms later on, the dead who rise in resurrection, the barefoot quester who is finally crowned) finds its analogues in both the outer world of nature (birds, bumblebees, hills) and the inner world of sense (hours, grief, eternity). Because this poem is representative and demonstrates clearly the sources to which the poet turned for symbolic figures, it is particularly useful as a pattern to order her imagery in the early poems. One may group images of motion (the things that *fly*), and of stasis (the things that *stay*), and of the bridging metamorphosis.

Emily Dickinson's private typology based upon visible aspects
of nature discloses a major distinction between her understanding of types and that of traditional Puritanism. The assertion by
G. F. Whicher is misleading: "The Puritan conception of nature
as a visible manifestation of God, which Jonathan Edwards and
Bryant in many of his early poems overtly expressed, was so
ingrained in [Emily Dickinson] that she took it for granted
without comment." [2] Certainly Emily Dickinson often draws a
direct analogy between natural phenomena and metaphysical
ideas. The seed-and-blossom metaphor is one of the clearest
examples; the poet uses it to signify the body in the grave and its
resurrection.

> When I count the seeds
> That are sown beneath,
> To bloom so, bye and bye–
>
> When I con the people
> Lain so low,
> To be received as high–
>
> When I believe the garden
> Mortal shall not see–
> Pick by faith it's blossom
> And avoid it's Bee,
> I can spare this summer, unreluctantly.

Emily Dickinson's use of typology is neither a naive and consistently direct correlation of the visible with the conjectured,
however, nor is it in other respects a Puritan usage. She inter-
posed a strong secularism in the Puritan habit of drawing analogues and the result was a greater objectivity on her part, an
awareness of the ironic possibilities within the language of metaphor, and a movement toward individual skepticism, in direct
contrast to the humility and acceptance which characterize Puritan usage. Of the English Puritan, Perry Miller writes: "In the
face of every experience he was obliged to ask himself, What

does this signify? And for furnishing significances, any event or object would do as well as any other, a pot or a pan, a rose or a lark — whatever made the meaning clearer was the better." [3] The purpose of Jonathan Edwards' manuscript entitled *Images or Shadows of Divine Things* was to clarify for his day the Puritan communal typology. According to Miller, Edwards addressed himself to this question: "If God is speaking through the rising sun or the flowering fruit tree, how can man be secure in understanding if God is saying several things at once?" [4] It is this need to codify nature's signals which Emily Dickinson does not pursue. She accepts, employs even, the ambiguity of meaning in her private typology, calling now upon metaphysical significations and now upon the intractable secular interpretations. This technique of equivocation parallels her use of the hymnal form to create occasions of irony. From what had been a narrowly construed religious typology she draws connotations of earthly concerns and attitudes of wit, irony, and rebellion.

As early as 1860, Emily Dickinson was aware in a sophisticated way that the habit of finding symbolic meaning in nature was a manifestation of mere self-deceit. In "Make me a picture of the sun" (P–188), for example, the skepticism is explicit:

> Make me a picture of the sun–
> So I can hang it in my room–
> And make believe I'm getting warm
> When others call it "Day"!
>
> Draw me a Robin–on a stem–
> So I am hearing him, I'll dream,
> And when the Orchards stop their tune–
> Put my pretense–away–
>
> Say if it's really–warm at noon–
> Whether it's Buttercups–that "skim"–
> Or Butterflies–that "bloom"?
> Then–skip–the frost–upon the lea–
> And skip the Russet–on the tree–
> Let's play those–never come!

She is aware one has a choice as to how he interprets the signs. And she is aware, too, that one has a choice as to which signs one cares to place his faith in, for if one wishes he may omit the deadly signs of autumn and of frost:

> Then–skip–the–frost–upon the lea–
> And skip the Russett–on the tree–
> Let's play those–never come!

In effect, and in distinct contrast to the Puritan acceptance of an affirmative typology, Emily Dickinson acknowledges in this poem that the meaning of nature's signs resides in the individual and is subject to whatever the individual cares to read into them. The interpreter may dismiss signs unsuited to what he cares to believe. In this attitude there is little naiveté, no unexamined exercise of a hand-me-down tradition, but rather skeptical questioning and a recognition that the phenomena of nature are pliable to her intentions, to her vision of reality, and to her notion of metaphysics. It is therefore a distortion of this poet's intentions to read her poems as if there were operating throughout a coherent and rigid system of typology. It is perhaps less misleading to view her imagery not as evidence of a *systematic* typology, but rather as figures from a store of analogies to which she returned repeatedly to objectify her own unique and often compounded attitudes.

The store from which she drew was an extensive one: nature as it revealed itself around her, the Bible, domestic life, the legal and the lapidary professions, the hierarchy of royalty, geography, the theater, the military, and even the spectacle of a balloon ascension. All of these sources (the list is not exhaustive) are apparent in the poetry of her early years. In such a profusion of figures, it is useful to arrange them generally in the terms of the poem "Some things that fly there be." The images, then, may be placed in three groups: those that depict the actual and evanescent, those that render the ideal and permanent, and those that convey the paradoxical combination of the two. In each regard the poet turns most often to sources which can be separated, for purposes of discussion, into the domestic, the cosmic, the familiar and natural, and the exotic and precious.

Of the early poems which concern themselves with "things that fly" and which acquire their imagery from domestic and cosmic sources, the four which follow are representative. The first, "She sweeps with many-colored Brooms" (P–219), has been discussed earlier; here the poem serves to demonstrate how Emily Dickinson transforms natural forces through the use of domestic imagery, creating an illusion of familiarity and intelligibility. The first stanza personifies nature as a housewife, and identifies the blowing leaves and debris with the dust and shreds in a house. The trees, waving their tinted leaves, are nature's brooms:

> She sweeps with many-colored Brooms–
> And leaves the Shreds behind–
> Oh Housewife in the Evening West–
> Come back, and dust the Pond!

The flying leaves are threads and scattered clothes which nature, now apostrophized, leaves behind:

> You dropped a Purple Ravelling in–
> You dropped an Amber thread–
> And now you've littered all the East
> With Duds of Emerald!

In a second representative work, "Delight is as the flight" (P–257), she yokes homely and cosmic imagery, rendering the mind's response to the phenomenon of a rainbow. The rainbow is described as

> A Skein
> Flung colored, after Rain.

The speaker declares it is the evanescent which has seemed to her the most persistent characteristic of the world around her:

> And I, for glee,
> Took Rainbows, as the common way,
> And empty Skies
> The eccentricity.

The resulting reflective mood of the speaker then produces at the close the lyrical response that fleeting things are the more precious for being transitory:

> And so with Lives–
> And so with Butterflies–
> Seen magic–through the fright
> That they will cheat the sight–
> And Dower latitudes far on–
> Some sudden morn–
> Our portion–in the fashion–
> Done.

Another poem illustrates her appropriation of the vastness of cosmic imagery to convey emotional states; it illustrates, too, the unassigned symbolism Emily Dickinson employs which defies precise interpretation. The two quatrains of "I lost a World–the other day!" (P–181) are elegiac. The apparent allusion to Christ's crown of thorns (here a "Row of Stars") suggests that it may be a person who has been lost:

> I lost a World–the other day!
> Has Anybody found?
> You'll know it by the Row of Stars
> Around it's forehead bound.
>
> A Rich man–might not notice it–
> Yet–to my frugal Eye,
> Of more Esteem than Ducats–
> Oh find it–Sir–for me!

If the intent is indeed elegiac, the second stanza fails the emotion by its use of the hackneyed imagery of wealth to establish the worth of the loss. In "If *He dissolve*–then–there is *nothing*–

more" (P–236), the cosmic (and here, too, Christian) imagery
does not offset the homely imagery to create effective tension
between the remote and the familiar, but rather gives way
finally to the trite and embarrassingly inconsistent depiction of a
dog and his master. The dark depth of intense grief is forcefully
depicted in the first two stanzas; they express a grief so profound
that for the bereft the normal motions of the universe seem to be
inverted:

> If *He dissolve–*then–there is *nothing–more–*
> *Eclipse–*at *Midnight–*
> It was *dark–before–*
>
> *Sunset–*at *Easter–*
> *Blindness–*on the *Dawn–*
> *Faint* Star of Bethlehem–
> *Gone down!*

This striking statement of despair is weakened by the commonplace metaphor in the final stanza:

> Say–that a *little life–*for *His–*
> Is *leaking–red–*
> His *little Spaniel–*tell Him!
> *Will He heed?*

However varied the success of its expression, her theme of aspiration for the fulfillment denied by separation persists.

Two poems show us how the poet turned for her imagery to
the objects and events of nature as they appeared in her New
England countryside. In "The Robin's my Criterion for Tune"
(P–285), Emily Dickinson's speaker recognizes that one most
naturally turns to the familiar for figurative language. The opening two lines draw the argument of the poem:

> The Robin's my Criterion for Tune–
> Because I grow–where Robins do.

The poet inventories the natural material about her — the butter-
cup, the orchard, the daisy, the October nut and the winter snow.

> The ode familiar–rules the Noon–
> The Buttercup's, my Whim for Bloom–
> Because, we're Orchard sprung–
> But, were I Britain born,
> I'd Daisies spurn–
> None but the Nut–October fit–
> Because, through dropping it,
> The Seasons flit–I'm taught–
> Without the Snow's Tableau
> Winter, were lie–to me.

The poem ends with the much-quoted lines which, we now see, have an ironic quality, since the poet did indeed draw material from beyond her own geographical province. The introduction of the "Queen" in the next to final line refers, one may suppose, to the creative impulse which for Emily Dickinson seemed to reside complete, lifelike, and somehow dissociated within her:

> Because I see–New Englandly–
> The Queen, discerns like me–
> Provincially.

Similar images recur elsewhere. The daisy, for a single example, appears in an earlier poem (P–106) as an analogue of the faithful companion:

> The Daisy follows soft the Sun–
> And when his golden walk is done–
> Sits shyly at his feet.

The "little spaniel" situation is implicit in the language here, but it is partially redeemed by the artfully subtle intensification of emotion, with its climax in the final lines:

> We are the Flower–Thou the Sun!
> Forgive us, if as days decline–
> We nearer steal to Thee!
> Enamored of the parting West–
> The peace–the flight–the Amethyst–
> Night's possibility!

An achievement of a much higher order is her imagistic rendering of a sunset (P–228). The poem illustrates the poet's fusion of the imagery of the precious and the exotic to objectify the magnificence of the spectacle. The first two lines indicate how she employs the connotations of the precious and the exotic (with the underlying fire metaphor) to vivify her picture. The sunset is seen

> Blazing in Gold and Quenching in Purple
> Leaping like Leopards to the Sky.

The effectiveness derives from the yoking of the images of fire, precious metal, and rich color, which form a splendid background for the striking figure of the leopards in flight.

The miscellany of images with which the poet expresses movement and the things that fly is extensive. Two poems will suggest this diversity and also her manner of appropriating figures to her intention. She employs military imagery, for example, to convey the intense impulse to escape out of oneself and the coincident recognition that one's power to do so is frustratingly feeble. The second quatrain of "I never hear the word 'escape'" (P–77) reads:

> I never hear of prisons broad
> By soldiers battered down,
> But I tug childish at my bars
> Only to fail again!

This manner in which Emily Dickinson creates emotion dissociated from explicit causal experience evoked from R. P. Blackmur the reaction that "we can feel the sentiment but we have lost the meaning."[5] She is more explicit about causation in "I've known a Heaven, like a Tent" (P–243), which takes its imagery from the traveling show:

> I've known a Heaven, like a Tent–
> To wrap it's shining Yards–
> Pluck up it's stakes, and disappear–
> Without the sound of Boards
> Or Rip of Nail–Or Carpenter–
> But just the miles of Stare–
> That signalize a Show's Retreat–
> In North America.

The feeling of irreversible separation (the "miles of Stare") seems to have as its cause the loss of religious faith, with the implication of mild satire on a religion that had been, even before its final dissolution, little more than a staged show. The poem declares heaven to have been a jerry-built affair as easily packed off as the collapsible devices of a traveling circus.

Emily Dickinson's obsessive concern with the things that flee, in nature and in one's life — the rainbow, the lover, the dead, faith — is translated through a broad range of imagery employed with an individuality clearly divergent from Puritan typology. Not only is the poet versatile and wide-ranging in selection, but she achieves a superior vividness and depth of statement through extreme concision and a unique, sometimes shocking, appropriation of both common and unexpected images to her intentions. In addition, her imagery for the things that fly contributes artfully to her metaphorical embodiment of that underside of her aspirational vision which is restless, doubt-ridden, continually thrusting toward the goal of self-fulfillment.

Her treatment of the things that "stay" is similarly managed through unique uses of imagery drawn in large part from the same sources — domestic, cosmic, the natural world, and the exotic and precious. She often combines within a single poem figures from distinct and seemingly unrelated sources. Archibald MacLeish has commented on this technique: the images, he says, "are in constant play and . . . their coupling is a coupling back and forth, not only between incongruities, but between worlds — the visible and the invisible." [6] Whicher remarks similarly in a useful statement which errs only in the attempt to trace her vision and consequent employment of imagery to her personal problems: "Her long struggle to face down frustration gave her a curious doubleness of vision, as though her two eyes did not make one in sight but, bird-like, were focussed in opposite directions, one upon the world of sense and one upon the world of changeless things. In her mind the two sets of images were sometimes whimsically blended, sometimes violently contrasted." [7]

Of poems which concern themselves with the things that "stay," the changeless materials in nature or in mind which operate to sustain one in the face of the things that fly, those which follow are representative. Domestic imagery, in particular the home itself (her frequent figure for security), symbolizes a sure and secular repose. In "Tho' I get home how late–how late" (P–207), the fire on the hearth and the waiting family represent the ultimate goal of reunion:

> Tho' I get home how late–how late–
> So I get home–'twill compensate–
> Better will be the Extasy
> That they have done expecting me–
> When Night–descending–dumb–and dark–
> They hear my unexpected knock–
> Transporting must the moment be–
> Brewed from decades of Agony!
>
> To think just how the fire will burn–
> Just how long-cheated eyes will turn–
> To wonder what myself will say,
> And what itself, will say to me–
> Beguiles the Centuries of way!

The image of the home persists in Emily Dickinson's thought in the early years. In a letter to her brother Austin in 1851 (L–59) she envisions a drama identical to that which the poem stages:

> You had a windy evening going back to Boston, and we thought

of you many times and hoped you would not be cold. Our fire burned so cheerfully I could'nt help thinking of how many were *here* and how many were away, and I wished so many times during that long evening that the door would open and you come walking in. Home is a holy thing — nothing of doubt or distrust can enter it's blessed portals. I feel it more and more as the great world goes on and one and another forsake, in whom you place your trust — here seems indeed to be a bit of Eden which not the sin of *any* can utterly destroy — smaller it is indeed, and it may be less fair, but fairer it is and brighter than all the world beside.[8]

To the extent that this familiar domestic situation is made to signify a condition of salvation, it accords with the Puritan tradition. Writing of the Puritan typology, Perry Miller asserts in his edition of Edwards' *Images or Shadows of Divine Things*: "The Puritan image had to be clearly applicable to the proposition, and it had to be drawn from a range of experience familiar to ordinary men."[9] But unlike the Puritan, Emily Dickinson occasionally effects telling satire on the orthodoxy of man's depravity. She employs in her homely metaphor not only the familiar but the playfully absurd, as in "Papa above!" (P–61):

> Papa above!
> Regard a Mouse
> O'erpowered by the Cat!
> Reserve within thy kingdom
> A "Mansion" for the Rat!
>
> Snug in seraphic Cupboards
> To nibble all the day,
> While unsuspecting Cycles
> Wheel solemnly away!

On this occasion, she is detached sufficiently from her controlling theme to use the opportunity for comedy.

One of her earliest poems (P–2), incorporated originally into the prose which closes a letter dated October 1851 to her brother Austin, exemplifies the way Emily Dickinson employed her nature imagery to typify the things that *stay* (in both senses of the word as she uses it):

> There is another sky,
> Ever serene and fair,
> And there is another sunshine,
> Though it be darkness there;
> Never mind faded forests, Austin,
> Never mind silent fields–
> *Here* is a little forest,
> Whose leaf is ever green;
> Here is a brighter garden,
> Where not a frost has been;
> In its unfading flowers
> I hear the bright bee hum;
> Prithee, my brother,
> Into *my* garden come!

There are other poems in which the staying power of nature is declared. In "Me, change! Me, alter!" (P–268) the declaration identifies the speaker with nature:

> Me, change! Me, alter!
> Then I will, when on the Everlasting Hill
> A Smaller Purple grows–
> At sunset, or a lesser glow
> Flickers upon Cordillera–
> At Day's superior close!

Nature lay always at hand as a repository for imagery, whether her particular intention in a poem was to explore what flees from life or what sustains by its permanence.

She employs the exotic or the foreign (as in the poem just cited) to suggest the things that are eternal and which sustain. In "Our lives are Swiss (P–80), Italy represents the longed-for but forever remote goal. Its signification is imprecise, suggesting almost any sort of wished-for terminal. The Alps, if immortality is taken to be the thematic frame, stand for the experience of death which separates one from the place of immortality. Within

other possible contexts the Alps may stand for any trial one must
endure before reaching a desired goal:

> Our lives are Swiss–
> So still–so Cool–
> Till some odd afternoon
> The Alps neglect their Curtains
> And we look farther on!
>
> *Italy* stands the other side!
> While like a guard between–
> The solemn Alps–
> The siren Alps
> Forever intervene!

Of poems in which the unchanging is expressed in an image
from her miscellaneous store, "What Inn is this" (P–115) is
representative. The inn and the "curious rooms" are a cemetery.
Her use of the imagery of hostelry provides the artful and
ironical emphasis of the utter cold and inactivity within the
tombs where the dead reside, forever denied activity and gaiety
and sound:

> What Inn is this
> Where for the night
> Peculiar Traveller comes?
> Who is the Landlord?
> Where the maids?
> Behold, what curious rooms!
> No ruddy fires on the hearth–
> No brimming Tankards flow–
> Necromancer! Landlord!
> Who are these below?

A majority of the early poems fall within the third of the
categories into which this discussion of imagery is organized. In
expressing the paradox of those that "resting, rise," the poet turns
again to the same store of images she employs in depicting the
transitory and the eternal. In "I'm 'wife'–I've finished that"

(P–199), for example, she juxtaposes the terms of marriage and sovereignty with cosmic imagery:

> I'm "wife"–I've finished that–
> That other state–
> I'm Czar–I'm "Woman" now–
> It's safer so–
>
> How odd the Girl's life looks
> Behind this soft Eclipse–

Nature images serve also to objectify this idea of metamorphosis. In a simple verse (P–25), another example where the speaker identifies herself with nature, the submerged seed metaphor provides an image for the awakening of spring:

> She slept beneath a tree–
> Remembered but by me.
> I touched her Cradle mute–
> She recognized the foot–
> Put on her carmine suit
> And see!

In a similar treatment of the identification of spring with the resurrection (P–74), Emily Dickinson employs the same imagery as that in the poem about her New England provinciality, combining with it the kind of domestic images she uses in "She sweeps with many-colored Brooms":

> A Lady red–amid the Hill
> Her annual secret keeps!
> A Lady white, within the Field
> In placid Lily sleeps!
>
> The tidy Breezes, with their Brooms —
> Sweep vale–and hill–and tree!
> Prithee, My pretty Housewives!
> Who may expected be?

> The Neighbors do not yet suspect!
> The Woods exchange a smile!
> Orchard, and Buttercup, and Bird–
> In such a little while!
>
> And yet, how still the Landscape stands!
> How nonchalant the Hedge!
> As if the "Resurrection"
> Were nothing very strange!

The unaccountable wonder of nature's annual resurrection is deprived of its mystery in the first three stanzas by the familiar imagery of the garden and the household. The fourth stanza abruptly reasserts the secret in that characteristic shift we have come to anticipate in the Dickinson strategy.

Of particular imagery to which the poet turns repeatedly in her early work to signify metamorphosis, no two instances seem more appropriate than the images of dawn changing into day and the caterpillar changing into the butterfly. Both most often embody the idea of the resurrection. In "Sleep is supposed to be" (P–13), for example, *dawn* obviously stands for nature's re-enactment of the resurrection. The final nine lines of this poem disclose the meaning:

> Morn is supposed to be
> By people of degree
> The breaking of the Day.
>
> Morning has not occurred!
>
> That shall Aurora be–
> East of Eternity–
> One with the banner gay–
> One in the red array–
> *That* is the break of Day!

As for the caterpillar analogy, the closing lines of "A fuzzy fellow, without feet" (P–173) indicate the poet's awareness that what she sees in the yearly emergence of the butterfly from the cocoon has a significance for her of specific meaning. The poem, referring to the caterpillar, concludes:

> But when winds alarm the Forest Folk,
> He taketh *Damask* Residence–
> And struts in sewing silk!
>
> Then, finer than a Lady,
> Emerges in the spring!
> A Feather on each shoulder!
> You'd scarce recognize him!
>
> By Men, yclept Caterpillar!
> By me! But who am I,
> To tell the pretty secret
> Of the Butterfly!

Other early poems which rely centrally on this evidence of metamorphosis in the image of the cocoon are "Cocoon above! Cocoon below!" (P–129) and "So from the mould" (P–66).

The persistence of kinetic and static imagery, separate and in combination in these representative poems from the early years, indicates Emily Dickinson's particular vision and the way in which she repeatedly formulated it. As early as 1859 she had defined the essential riddle of movement, stasis, and metamorphosis which was to compel her attention throughout the formative period. The statement of this central concern appears in the poem "Some things that fly there be." A large and significant body of her early work can be organized through the perspective which this poem provides. The poem also helps to draw the reader's attention to the movement which informs so much of her poetry. Where she is particularly successful, she combines imagery from seemingly disparate sources, and by so doing creates out of the incongruity not only a vital sense of movement but also a tension artfully appropriate to the emotional activity concomitant with the quest for self-fulfillment.

But no discussion of Emily Dickinson's imagery would fairly

represent her technique without directing attention to the problem of interpretation posed by the shifting symbolic values of her images. She was aware of the profusion of interpretive extensions which variously arise and radiate from her poetry. Some poems from the later period help define the problem as it exists in the work of the formative period. In the later poem beginning "Could mortal lip divine" (P–1409), she acknowledges the broad connotative power of language. The poem itself is a good example of what she is talking about:

> Could mortal lip divine
> The undeveloped Freight
> Of a delivered syllable
> 'Twould crumble with the weight.

An effective ambiguity hovers over the subject of the verb "crumble." The syntax suggests first that a single word is capable of carrying a burden of meaning far out of proportion to the magnitude of the utterance. This same understanding of the power of language in poetry is implied in the first quatrain of "I dwell in Possibility" (P–657):

> I dwell in Possibility–
> A fairer House than Prose–
> More numerous of Windows–
> Superior–for Doors.

A similar recognition informs the poem beginning "Shall I take thee, the Poet said / to the propounded word?" (P–1126). In the closing quatrain the poet acknowledges the immensity of the poetic vision for which the word can be only an indication:

> That portion of the Vision
> The Word applied to fill
> Not unto nomination
> The Cherubim reveal.

The second possibility in the ambiguous subject of "crumble" evolves from the syntax if the subject of this verb is "lip." Such an arrangement then suggests that the reader, divining the full intended meaning of a word, must see so directly into the vision as to be affected emotionally and to show that emotion in a facial gesture. This idea of the affective force of words is the burden of the poem beginning "A Word dropped careless on a Page" (P–1261). Here, the poet says, the power of language is so great that if used indiscriminately it may thereafter instill despair in the divining reader, even after the poet is dead and folded within the perpetual seam of the grave:

> A Word dropped careless on a Page
> May stimulate an eye
> When folded in perpetual seam
> The Wrinkled Maker lie
>
> Infection in the sentence breeds
> We may inhale Despair
> At distances of Centuries
> From the Malaria–

The opening line of "Could mortal lip divine," the poem with which this discussion opened, is itself suggestive of the divine power of the poet who, in the metaphor of another late poem (P–1247), can create a force like thunder. It is the mortal poet, she implies in her verbal trick, whose lip (the ability to create in language) is divine. This view is reaffirmed in the poem beginning "The Brain–is wider than the Sky" (P–632). That poem at the end equates the mortal brain and God, the significant distinction between the two being that God works through silent revelation, whereas the poet reveals through language:

> The Brain is just the weight of God–
> For–Heft them–Pound for Pound–
> And they will differ–if they do–
> As Syllable from Sound.

This possibility for numerous extensions from certain of her "freighted" words is a marked characteristic of Emily Dickinson's poetry. R. P. Blackmur speaks of the Dickinson manner as "the compactness of that which is unexpanded and depends for context entirely upon its free implication." [10] He isolates precisely the difficulty in arriving at definitive readings for a number of the Dickinson poems. The reader, in other words, lacking precise contextual direction provided by the poem itself, brings to it his casual inferences, and, in effect, is compelled often to give symbols a reading rooted in his own experience. Here is the verbal equivalent of *sfumato*, the technique in expressionistic painting whereby information (color and line) on a canvas is given only piecemeal and thereby necessarily stimulates the imaginative projection of the viewer, who, out of his own experience, supplies the missing contours and, ultimately, the context.

For certain of Emily Dickinson's favorite images, the difficulty of interpretation increases as one's knowledge of her work broadens. An example of the way in which she attaches a number of possible meanings to images and symbols is her use of the sea image. Again, the late poems provide an entering wedge to the early ones. In "I started Early–Took my Dog" (P–520), the sea is death objectified, and the closing two stanzas visualize the speaker's encounter with death as a walk by the seaside:

> And He–He followed–close behind–
> I felt His Silver Heel
> Upon my Ancle–Then my Shoes
> Would overflow with Pearl–
>
> Until We met the Solid Town–
> No One He seemed to know–
> And bowing–with a Mighty look–
> At me–The Sea withdrew.

"Fortitude incarnate" (P–1217) also asserts the power and deadliness of the sea:

> Edifice of Ocean
> Thy tumultuous Rooms
> Suit me at a venture
> Better than the Tombs.

"Water makes many Beds" (P–1428) ponders the possibility that watery death entails the horror of eternal restlessness.

> Water makes many Beds
> For those averse to sleep–
> It's awful chamber open stands–
> It's Curtains blandly sweep–
> Abhorrent is the Rest
> In undulating Rooms
> Whose Amplitude no end invades–
> Whose Axis never comes.

In poems of the formative years, the sea is symbolic of life's stormy condition in which one looks for a haven. A very early work (P–4) discloses this meaning:

> On this wondrous sea
> Sailing silently,
> Ho! Pilot, ho!
> Knowest thou the shore
> Where no breakers roar–
> Where the storm is o'er?
>
> In the peaceful west
> Many the sails at rest–
> The anchors fast–
> Thither I pilot *thee*–
> Land Ho! Eternity!
> Ashore at last!

And the same meaning is associated with the sea setting in the first stanza of "Adrift! A little boat adrift!" (P–30):

> Adrift! A little boat adrift!
> And night is coming down!
> Will *no* one guide a little boat
> Unto the nearest town? [11]

Other early efforts represent the sea as a symbol of fulfillment, and more specifically, of fulfillment through love. Two poems are representative of this type in the Dickinson canon. The first is "My River runs to thee" (P–162):

> My River runs to thee–
> Blue Sea! Wilt welcome me?
> My River waits reply–
> Oh Sea–look graciously–
> I'll fetch thee Brooks
> From spotted nooks–
> *Say*–Sea– Take *Me*!

The second poem (P–284) most clearly, through the reference to the wife of the sea god, suggests that fulfillment in love is the subject:

> The Drop, that wrestles in the Sea–
> Forgets her own locality–
> As I–toward Thee–
>
> She knows herself an incense small–
> Yet *small*–she sighs–if *All*–is *All*–
> How *larger*–be?
>
> The Ocean–smiles–at her Conceit–
> But *she*, forgetting Amphitrite–
> Pleads–"Me"?

If in a number of poems like the well-known "Wild Nights– Wild Nights!" the possible meanings radiate out from the basic image, perhaps sometimes even diffusing the effect, there are other poems in which the multiple connotations combine in one powerfully complex image. A poem as early as 1859, "Went up a year this evening!" (P–93), demonstrates unmistakably the mature facility with which this poet early in her career was able to synthesize effects into a single intense and complex expression. Most interesting in the light of the preceding discussion of the free implication of her language is the artful way she appropriates for her own purposes the inferences the reader necessarily extracts from the limited contextual situation she provides. That is, she seems to anticipate the reader's reactions and counterpoints them. If the reader is repeatedly disconcerted and made to rearrange his mental image, he is ultimately satisfied by the final coherence of the disparate elements.

The first two lines of the poem set the scene for a New Year celebration:

> Went up a year this evening!
> I recollect it well!

Immediately and contrary to the expectations, there is shown to be a grotesque silence in the crowd:

> Amid no bells nor bravoes
> The bystanders will tell!

The mystery is compounded in the next lines in which this rising year is personified:

> Cheerful—as to the village—
> Tranquil—as to repose—
> Chastened—as to the Chapel
> This humble Tourist rose!

The personification in combination with "repose" and "Chapel" (terms which to Emily Dickinson as often as not suggested death) injects here the suspicion that something besides the year has departed. The next lines, however, provide a fresh suggestion which, by its seeming whimsicality, works in counterpoint to the solemn scene:

> Did not talk of returning!
> Alluded to no time
> When, were the gales propitious—
> We might look for him!

The rising imagery now, and the reference to wind, combine to create the spectacle of a balloon ascension. Lines further on confirm this interpretation:

> Hands bustled at the moorings–
> The crowd respectful grew–
> Ascended from our vision
> To Countenances new!

Reading the poem now in the knowledge that death (of a year? a person?) is the subject being obliquely formulated, the moorings become ambiguously the handling ropes of a balloon and the cords attached to a coffin to lower it into the grave. The silence of the crowd is explained: they are mourners. Yet the rising balloon metaphor connotes gaiety, and one can then see this image as the objectification of the ascending spirit, cheerfully wobbling up to heaven as to the "village." This same juxtaposition of the whimsical and the solemn appears in her only other poem employing the image of a balloon ascension. In "You've seen Balloons set–Hav'nt You?" (P–700) the second and third stanzas read:

> Their Liquid Feet go softly out
> Upon a Sea of Blonde–
> They spurn the Air, as 'twere too mean
> For Creatures so renowned–
>
> Their Ribbons just beyond the eye–
> They struggle–some–for Breath–
> And yet the Crowd applaud, below–
> They would not encore–Death.

The poem "Went up a year this evening!," that began as a New Year celebration, ends with the unmistakable image of death:

> A Difference–A Daisy–
> Is all the rest I knew!

This poem illustrates the mature artistry of the poet who was still to pose three years later in her letters to Higginson as an artless versifier in search of a preceptor. There is created in this poem that vivid sense of motion which enlivened her poetry and, indeed, was the central metaphor by which she apprehended experience. Her mature skill in "Went up a year this evening!" has created the precise yet paradoxical sense of motion working in opposite directions. The poem embodies the sort of achievement one finds in Herbert's "The Collar," where the spirit soars up even while the flesh proclaims its descent. Emily Dickinson's poem illustrates also her psychological insight, here into the reaction of the spectators at a funeral, inwardly excited as at a balloon ascension or a New Year wassail, yet outwardly silent and solemn at the spectacle of death. These disparate images of celebration, of carnival spectacle, and of a funeral gathering coalesce finally to recreate the experience of the muted entertainment that a funeral provides, and, at the same time, to recreate the mixed emotions of the individual in the funeral crowd who may coincidentally enjoy the spectacle while he fears for his own mortality. Emily Dickinson echoes the wisdom of the messenger of death in Everyman: "Look well, and take good heed to the ending, be you never so gay!"

Finally, the direction of her early artistry is apparent in the way she manipulates the free implications that her poetry evokes. The contextual vagueness which Blackmur notes may become for Emily Dickinson a virtue. The undeveloped freight of her syllables is ultimately gathered into a coherent and complex rendering of emotional paradoxes. Her imagery in the early poetry repeatedly embodies motion, rest, and metamorphosis, the encompassing metaphor in turn manifesting appropriately her central thematic concern with the polar states of the actual and the ideal and the *act* of aspiring from the one to the other state. Like her metrical forms and her ambivalent speaker, her imagery is appropriate to her intention. That this propriety exists in the early work is evidence of the artistry of both her poetic conception and execution.

The final paradox resists resolution, however. While she delighted in drawing the forms and appearances of the natural world, she was fundamentally neither confident nor intimate with it. As often as her imagery suggests a cozy harmony with the world, it records with a terrifying simplicity the wracking condition of gratification denied, passion unreturned, and understanding thwarted.

AUDIBLE CORRELATIVES OF
EMOTIONAL TENSION

The freedom and inventiveness with which Emily Dickinson relates sounds in her early verse are also significant qualities of her style and evidence of her early independence as an artist. Her rhyming method does not seem to be neglect or laxity of the poetic art, as G. F. Whicher suggests when he says that Emily Dickinson "accepted inexact rhymes because their hinted tinkling served to round her stanzas as well as fully chiming syllables."[1] Indeed, the effectiveness and persistence of her novel rhymes must lead us to acknowledge that she was not merely satisfied with approximate rhyme; rather, she was a bold poet actively and deliberately intent upon creating unique patterns outside convention. Nor does her manner of manipulating sound seem simply a willful disregard of form which Higginson saw as a principal characteristic of her work. In an *Atlantic Monthly* article of 1891, this man who was the first of her critics, in referring to the early poem "Your riches taught me poverty" (P–299), declared: "Here was already manifest that defiance of form, never through carelessness, and never precisely from whim, which so marked her."[2] Nor still is her manner of composition evidence of a necessity to sacrifice conventional form in the effort to give adequate verbal expression to the arc of her thought. This view is presented by Gay Wilson Allen: "She often had to sacrifice versification for a closely-packed metaphor or a barbed epigram, not because she had any intention of breaking the conventional rules but because what she had to say did not precisely fit the accentuation and form which the conventional scheme demanded."[3] This judgment would ignore the formal poetic boundaries within which Emily Dickinson worked and which consistently contained her ingenuity. To say that she wrote outside the primary bounds of poetic form is, after all, to say that she wrote prose. This is clearly not true.[4]

Rather, we should recognize that the poet was artfully modifying a received poetic schema, in particular Victorian mellifluousness, to suit her purposes, yet rarely allowing her work to deteriorate into formless prosaic expression. Her variations on convention demonstrate the mode of composition which Ernst Gombrich, in *Art and Illusion*, describes as "the long road through schema and correction."[5] She gave new life to the conventional forms of hymnody by informing them with novel characteristics which, in addition, perform the subtle alteration necessary to articulate her particular vision. A whole spectrum of rhyme variations, of individualistic modes of relating sounds, is a principal means by which this poet modified the received forms, animated them, and related them intimately to her meaning.

The problem of how much meaning the reader is justified in deriving from sound alone need not impede an analysis of the contribution Emily Dickinson's rhyme variations make to her meaning. René Wellek's and Austin Warren's tactful commentary on the theoretical problem is helpful here. Their discussion of the problems of determining the functions of sound rightly emphasizes that while word sounds (except for clearly onomatopoeic words) and sound correlations have no inherent meaning, they do acquire meaning and operate significantly in the individual poetic work:

Rhyme is an extremely complex phenomenon. It has its mere euphonious function as a repetition (or near-repetition) of sounds . . . But, though this sound-side may be basic, it is obviously only one aspect of rhyme. Aesthetically far more important is its metrical function signaling the conclusion of a line of verse, or as the organizer, sometimes the sole organizer, of stanzaic patterns. But, most important, rhyme has meaning and is thus deeply involved in the whole character of a work of poetry.[6]

The particular problems involved in the use and function of approximate rhyme are perhaps more vexing since few major poets have employed the device. D. S. R. Welland, in his study of the poetry of Wilfred Owen, believes but four poets have done so. The deliberate use of half-rhyme, he asserts, "is to be found in three poets before Owen: Henry Vaughan, Gerard Manley Hopkins, and Emily Dickinson."[7] Welland finds occasional use of approximate rhyme in Welsh poetry and in some of the work of Jules Romains.[8] The analyst of Emily Dickinson's rhyme variations, clearly, has no significant body of convention with which to make comparison, yet one can formulate with considerable confidence the functions of her relatively unique sounds and ultimately judge the significance of the technique within the larger visionary aspects of her art.

Of particular note, especially in view of the critical commentary on Emily Dickinson's near-rhymes, are her uses of exact rhyme and the frequency with which she employs it. In the early poetry the instances of exact rhyme as part of a recurrent pattern are considerably more numerous than general critical assertions indicate. Thomas H. Johnson, for example, in discussing Emily Dickinson's use of identical, vowel, imperfect, and suspended rhymes concludes that "she selected [these rhymes] at will, singly or in combination, and she carried her freedom to the utmost limit by feeling no compulsion to use one rhyming pattern in a poem more than she felt constrained to use a single metric form."[9] Characteristically, of course, she does not follow a conventional rhyme pattern with the *x, a, x, a* disposition of identical sounds (which her persistent use of the hymn quatrain would suggest). But this is not reason to assume she has no individual scheme which recurs in her verse. For if one notes the frequency with which the first occasion of rhyme in individual early poems is an exact rhyme, it becomes apparent that a basic pattern is repeatedly employed. Of the three hundred and one poems from the early years, one hundred seventy-eight (well over half) have as their first rhyme an exact duplication of sound.[10] This pattern is represented in "'Heaven'–is what I cannot reach!" (P–239), where the exact rhyme in the first stanza is followed in the second stanza by three instances of suspended rhyme and in the third and final stanza by a vowel rhyme. The effect, indeed if not the intention, of such a persistent pattern in which the initial rhyme is exact, is to condition the ear first, to sensitize it to sound so that the sensory effort thereafter is in anticipation of subsequent instances of exact rhyme. Once sensitized, the ear makes an extraordinary effort to relate sounds, and is consequently receptive to a greater range and subtlety of sound relationships. Expectation is induced, then subtly denied. The technique accomplishes with sound a heightened responsiveness similar to that which the gathering of disparate images evokes.

Other persistent qualities of rhyme characterize the early poetry, and their recognition puts into proper perspective the extent to which Emily Dickinson freed herself from conventional use of exact rhyme. My method has been to take account of clear instances of exact rhyme and all other instances where even the remotest relationship between sounds is reinforced by the poet's general tendency to rhyme alternating lines. Vowel rhymes (die-me) for example, which might at first escape notice, often seem to be dictated by line arrangement. Instances where sounds echo back to an end-word several lines before are counted as occasions of rhyme when the identification seems to be a clear and intended one. Of course, to talk about rhyme as a statistical matter, without precise reference to particular functions in individual poems, has only a limited value. Nevertheless, what can be discerned in the way of general tendencies and of persistent technical habits is useful.

It is apparent that Emily Dickinson's use of exact rhyme is much more persistent than is generally suspected. It constitutes over half of the nearly twelve hundred occasions of rhyme in the early three hundred one poems. Yet from the further evidence of its relatively infrequent use *in sequence,* that is, its characteristic appearance in isolated instances, we find exact rhyme functions less as an element of regular formal patterning than as an element of technical virtuosity working inseparably from the other forms of rhyme which the poet uses. Her general store of rhyme types, ranging from exact rhyme to the more remote sound associations, are exact rhyme, suspended rhyme (*plot-foot*: identical terminal consonants following unlike vowels), imperfect rhyme (*foot-full*: identical vowel sounds terminated by unlike consonants), and vowel rhyme (*die-me*: unlike terminal vowels).[11] The more general terms *assonance* and *consonance* are used here to denote vowel and consonant sound correlation between syllables in words which do not end lines. Identical rhymes allow for no range of variation in the identity of sound, and eye rhymes may, depending upon the sounds, be placed in the suspended-, imperfect-, or vowel-rhyme categories. Consequently, neither identical nor eye rhymes are pertinent to the discussion here of the spectrum of word sound associations. Within each of the other categories, however, there exists a still finer procession of sounds, and this more subtle range, from close to remote identity of sound, serves to order in greater detail the breadth of the poet's rhyme usages.

The technical device of suspended rhyme accounts for slightly more than a fourth of the total number of rhyme occasions in the poet's early work. It is a mode of sound association next closest in auditory correspondence to the exact rhyme. In Emily Dickinson's usage, there are at least five degrees of identity within this category, from the closer association of sound to the

more distant. The poet employs simple terminal consonant likeness to achieve the closer sound relationships. Examples of this
type are *join-wine* (P–130) and the line-ending syllables in
the early (and otherwise uninteresting) "Angels, in the early
morning" (P–94), where the rhyme shifts support the movement denoted by the verbs:

> Angels, in the early morning
> May be seen the Dews among,
> Stooping–plucking–smiling–flying–
> Do the Buds to them belong?

At a slightly further remove are cases of suspended rhyme where
the vowels which precede the final relating consonants vary in
length. For example, one finds these words paired: *blood-atti-
tude* (P–77), *asleep-lip* (P–182), *between-on* (P–204), *then-
lain* (P–205). Where adroitly used, as in "A slash of Blue" (P–
204), this difference in vowel length functions in the movement
of the verse. In the two lines,

> A little purple–slipped between–
> Some Ruby Trowsers hurried on–

where the poet is creating a metaphorical image of an evening
sky, the shorter length of *on* contributes to the more active
movement connoted by *hurried*. A still more remote identification of sound occurs when, as in *Hedge-strange* pairing (P–74),
the final consonance is immediately preceded by other strongly
contrasting consonant sounds.

> And yet, how still the Landscape stands!
> How nonchalant the Hedge!
> As if the "Resurrection"
> Were nothing very strange!

The disparity in sound conveys audibly the observation of
strangeness toward which the poem builds in the final lines.
This sound association is slightly more remote than, for example,

word pairings where the double consonants have an identical sound, as in *cells-feels* (P–272) or *toils-smiles* (P–273). At a greater remove from this relatively close identification are pairs and groups of words where different sounds (in these cases "s" and "z") are crowded together and where the significantly operative sound does not necessarily fall at the end of the word, as in *Crucifix-guess-size* and *face-Paradise-ours* (P–225):

> Jesus! thy Crucifix
> Enable thee to guess
> The smaller size!
>
> Jesus! thy second face
> Mind thee in Paradise
> Of our's!

The double sounds here are sufficiently emphatic to help render the idea of the two states of mortality and immortality, and their combination appropriately underlies the idea of the fusion of both states in the figure of Christ. Sound shifts operate effectively, too, in "An awful Tempest mashed the air" (P–198), particularly in the final stanza where nature is depicted in the alteration from a night's storm to the calm of morning. *Arose-eyes-coast-peace-Paradise* suggest audibly that visual change:

> The morning lit–the Birds arose–
> The Monster's faded eyes
> Turned slowly to his native coast–
> And peace–was Paradise!

Effective use of some of these various modes of identifying sounds is apparent in the poem "Come slowly–Eden!" (P–211), where the consonance of "r" and "z" sounds (together, to be sure, with alliteration within the lines) reproduces by onomatopoeia the presence of the bee and, formally, serves to bind the four lines of the final stanza:

> Reaching late his flower,
> Round her chamber hums–
> Counts his nectars–
> Enters–and is lost in Balms.

The terminal words *flower* and *nectars* are bound by the "r" sound in the unstressed syllables, while the "z" sound in *nectars* binds it to both *hums* and *Balms*. Finally, *hums* and *Balms,* while not creating an exact rhyme, make a recognizable association of sound in the double consonant. These line-end devices reinforce the sound patterns established within the lines: like the poem "A Route of Evanescence" (P–1463), this earlier poem audibly conveys the sense of movement and sound in nature.

Imperfect rhymes make up a small portion of the rhyme occasions Emily Dickinson employs, but the type takes its place in the spectrum of sound devices only slightly more remote than suspended rhyme. Imperfect rhyme is basically an instance of assonance occurring in the line-ending word. It may take the form of pairs of words such as *cheek-speech* (P–208) or *run-come* (P–214). This variety of sound association is found in "Savior! I've no one else to tell" (P–217), where the intent is to express the difficulty of containing intense emotion ("the imperial Heart"). The sense of the speaker's difficulty is artfully provided with an auditory correlative in the line-end words:

> Nor, for myself, I came so far–
> That were the little load–
> I brought thee the imperial Heart
> I had not strength to hold.

The effort to hold the burden of the emotion which the speaker lays before the "Savior" is reintroduced in the effort the reader makes to achieve a full identity of sounds in *far-Heart* and *load-hold*. Vowel likeness is accurately created, but a consonant is left hovering; that is, there is no corresponding consonant sound for the final "t" in *Heart*, and the corresponding sound for the "l" in *hold* is only circuitously got at, appearing at the beginning of the rhyming word *load*. The shifting and awkward movement of sound makes audible representation of the awkward burden of great emotion.

Emily Dickinson's vowel rhymes constitute another area of the sound spectrum, at a still greater remove from conventional exact rhyme. Her relatively frequent use of this type (about one in twelve rhyme occasions and a device used only less frequently than exact or suspended rhyme in her early work) raises the questions of how she intended her syllable stresses to fall and to what extent, if any, the organ accompaniment to hymnody might have influenced this technique of vowel rhyme. That she was consciously employing this tenuous sound association is clear from poems such as "Sleep is supposed to be" (P–13) and "Just lost, when I was saved!" (P–160). In the earlier poem, for example, the three lines of the first stanza end this way:

> Sleep is supposed to be
> By souls of sanity
> The shutting of the eye.

The first two words form an exact rhyme, but the corresponding sound in *eye* occurs only in the second half of the diphthong. An exact rhyme here seems to be compelled by the multiple rhymes (*grand-hand-stand* and *gay-array-Day*) in the remainder of the poem.

> Sleep is the station grand
> Down wh', on either hand
> The hosts of witness stand!
>
> Morn is supposed to be
> By people of degree
> The breaking of the Day.
>
> Morning has not occurred!

> That shall Aurora be–
> East of Eternity–
> One with the banner gay–
> One in the red array–
> *That* is the break of Day!

In the later example, "Just lost, when I was saved!" the third stanza reads:

> Next time, to stay!
> Next time, the things to see
> By Ear unheard,
> Unscrutinized by Eye.

Lines one, two, and four create a complex form of rhyme in the diphthongs in *stay* and *eye*. The harmony occurs between the unstressed portions of the diphthongs. The sound identity is just tenuous enough to orchestrate the speaker's fleeting glimpse of eternity. Other instances of this form of sound association are numerous: *now-so* (P–199), *die-me* (P–205), *hoe-too* (P–215), *shoe-do-know* (P–229), *sky-day* (P–274). Emily Dickinson is not indiscriminate in her use of the vowel rhyme, for she rarely combines diphthong vowels in which neither portion of the diphthong has a corresponding sound. Where she does, other factors are sometimes at work visually to effect an identification. For example, in "When we stand on the tops of Things" (P–242), she pairs *flaw-away*. The diphthong sound correspondence is replaced by the visual correspondence of *aw*.[12] Where she employs disparate vowel sounds, she is able to effect a correspondence in deceiving the ear by way of the eye.

To read poems in which these diphthong correspondences occur, where we feel compelled to stress each portion of the diphthong strongly and equally, induces the speculation that perhaps the steady thump of the beats in hymns as they were sung by vigorous congregations was pulsing in the poet's ear. We know from experience, for example, the way in which a church congregation, as it comes to the final word of each hymn verse, gives the last part of a diphthong unnatural amplitude in that habitual stress designed to carry the rhythm over to the next verse. However Emily Dickinson came by this persistent use of vowel rhyme, her employment of it is closely related to her intention. It operates particularly well in "'Tis so appalling–it exhilirates" (P–281), a poem about confrontation with death and the consequent grotesque release from fearful speculation the speaker feels. Looking at death, the poet says, is like dying. After such an experience

> Others, Can wrestle–
> Your's is done–
> And so of Wo, bleak dreaded–come,
> It sets the Fright at liberty–
> And Terror's free–
> Gay, Ghastly, Holiday!

There is just enough distortion between the sound of *Holiday* and both *liberty* and *free*, and just the precise amount of disparity between the final stresses, to create the auditory correlative of the uneasy emotional holiday the speaker experiences after witnessing the look of death. The poem communicates the unnerving crosscurrents of resignation and fear as they alternately elate and terrify the observer.

Emily Dickinson's employment of varied rhyme constructs in the early poetry seems to sanction the inference that her ingenuity in this regard emerged not by chance or whimsy or by compromise of the poetic art but through a conscious deliberation. Effectiveness, we are aware, is not always at a high level, but where the achievement is superior these various unique departures from received rhyme tradition serve real and remarkably artful functions. These techniques of rhyme vitalize the formal hymn metrical patterns through which she works, and they also provide a technical correlative of that mode of vision manifest in her artistic expression. As Anderson notes in a brief reference to this technique, "the partial or tangential echo more nearly fit the steady tensions of her doubts and beliefs." [13] But in addition, the variations in rhyme function to overcome the monotony of the hymn forms she uses. She could not but be aware of the inherent monotony of the hymn form, a major difficulty Saintsbury defines when he observes of the forms based upon regular syllabic counts that their "rigid observance of the syllabic system produces, and cannot but produce, an intolerable monotony." [14]

In "I've known a Heaven, like a Tent" (P–243), discussed earlier in another connection, the occasions of suspended rhyme serve to counterpoint slightly varied sounds against the exactly regular common meter syllabic system in which the first stanza is composed. A similar employment of approximate rhyme occurs in " 'Heaven'–is what I cannot reach!" (P–239), where it not only vitalizes the regularity of the common meter form, but provides in addition an auditory correlation to the statement the poem makes about the abyss separating man from his visionary goal. The occasion for rhyme in the first stanza is exact:

> "Heaven"–is what I cannot reach!
> The Apple on the Tree–
> Provided it do hopeless–hang–
> That–"Heaven" is– to Me!

The tendency toward metrical regularity here is upset by the substitution of a trochee in the first line and a spondee in the fourth line. In the final stanza, where the iambic movement is regular, the rhyme approximation creates variety, at the same time contributing to the meaning of the statement the poem makes:

> Her teazing Purples–Afternoons–
> The credulous–decoy–
> Enamored–of the Conjuror–
> That spurned us–Yesterday!

"Her" refers to nature, personified and described as wearing

"Purples" in the afternoon light. The beauty of nature seems to be an intimation of Heaven, a "decoy" for the mortal observer. The distortion in sound (following the sensitizing exact rhyme in the first stanza) between *decoy* and *Yesterday* is sufficiently emphatic to establish audibly the disparity between the promise of the "teazing Purples" and the fact of the indicting God, the conjuror-creator who "spurned us." Ultimately, the poem argues that nature typifies the ideal which for the speaker is forever unattainable.

Certain of Emily Dickinson's structural patterns contribute their own sort of rigidity to an already highly rigid form. The poet often starkly declares in her first line the idea which rules the rest of the expression which follows. As Johnson says in his critical biography, "As she always does in her best poems, Emily Dickinson makes her first lines lock all succeeding lines into position."[15] In another commentary, he calls our attention to another habitual structural device of the poet: "The wheel horses of her stanzas are always the final lines, whether the poem is written as a series of quatrains or as a combination of stanza patterns."[16] His metaphor can be taken to mean that often the last lines perform the effective work, that is, they verify most clearly the sense in which the poem's idea is to be taken. The more general observation we might make is that Emily Dickinson characteristically structures her poems with sharp verbal surfaces self-reflecting and consequently self-illuminating, capable of fixing securely the reader's attention. An example will demonstrate this recurrent technique and demonstrate, too, the service that approximate rhyme performs in effecting a variation or audible counterpoint to the formal regularity. The poem "Alone, I cannot be" (P–298) records the speaker's feeling of being constantly attended by ghostly presences ("The Hosts"), perhaps the poetic impulse personified. Exact rhymes and suspended rhymes in the first two stanzas underline the regularity of the general iambic movement:

> Alone, I cannot be–
> The Hosts–do visit me–
> Recordless Company–
> Who baffle Key–
>
> They have no Robes, nor Names–
> No Almanacs–nor Climes–
> But general Homes
> Like Gnomes.

With the ear thus attuned by the insistent rhymes, the reader then comes to the final stanza:

> Their Coming, may be known
> By Couriers within–
> Their going–is not–
> For they're never gone.

The striking absence of rhyme in the third line obtrudes directly, confirming the absolute reality of the accompanying hosts. In the final line, in which suspended rhyme occurs between *gone* and *within*, the disparity in sound echoes the negation in the previous line.

Emily Dickinson's use of a variety of rhyme constructs, then, contributes a satisfying complexity to an otherwise rigid and fundamentally simple metrical form. They can be effective in drawing the reader's attention to the crucial statement. And in the same way that she sometimes creates images in the reader's mind only to transform them or combine them in novel arrangements, she employs rhyme to establish expectations of sound only to increase the effectiveness when she departs from the pattern. This is to say, finally, that rhyme is intimately related and artistically appropriate not only to her formal arrangements, but also to her meaning.

Approximate rhyme also helps create the illusion of conversational fidelity. In the poem "One Year ago–jots what?" (P–296), the speaker is trying to recapture (through the imagination) and to define an earlier time when parting from a lover was comparable to the pain of death:

> One Year ago–jots what?
> God–spell the word! I–cant–
> Was't Grace? Not that–
> Was't Glory? That–will do–
> Spell slower–Glory.

In a manner similar to Donne's and Browning's (the abruptness of the rhythm, the use of colloquial language, the implication that a listener is present), Emily Dickinson establishes a vivid sense of presence and of personality. Faithful to the experience of hearing a person speak out of great emotion, the poet here implies that the emotional pressure defies any sort of auditory or rhythmical regularity. In the final stanza, true to the emotional intensity, the end-sounds shift nervously, repel, effect an exact rhyme once (*then-Ten*), and terminate in the sound *None*, for which there has been no precise auditory preparation, and for the meaning of which, indeed, there has been only a subtly indicative tendency in the speaker's increasing insight into her condition:

> If to be "Elder"–mean most pain–
> I'm old enough, today, I'm certain–then–
> As old as thee–how soon?
> One–Birthday more–or Ten?
> Let me–choose!
> Ah, Sir, None!

In a more comprehensive sense, Emily Dickinson's frequent use of inexact rhyme creates a counterpoint of worldliness to the tonal connotations of the ideal associated with the hymn form. Like the creation of irony already noted in the discussion of metrics (the intrusion of the self, the secular desires, the introduction of the actual and the discordant into the apparent formal context of order, harmony, and faith), the intrusion of discordant sounds makes audible the noises of this less-than-perfect world as against the formal perfection of exact rhyme correspondence.[17] A striking example of this counter-pointing of the actual against the ideal has already been treated in the discussion of the poem "I've known a Heaven, like a Tent" (P–243). Faith has vanished, leaving the speaker with only the prospect of earthly time and place, with "just the miles of Stare" and the blank feeling that the prospect of heaven was never more permanent than a traveling show. The function of discordant sound in returning the gaze from the ideal to the present and actual — that is, the function of *sound disparities as sound correlatives of reality* — occurs also in "If I'm lost–now" (P–256). The speaker is reflecting on the loss of grace. She has experienced faith:

> The Angels–softly peered–
> And touched me with their fleeces,
> Almost as if they cared.

But loss of faith has occurred and the consequent banishment:

> I'm banished–now–you know it–
> How foreign that can be–
> You'll know–Sir–when the Savior's face
> Turns so–away from you.

The turning away from the ideal to the actual is sharply reflected in the sound disparity. Having been prepared by previous rhyme for a correspondence in sounds in the last and third from last lines, the reader encounters the grating disparity between *be* and *you*; the occasion becomes the sound image of despair. The image occurs inevitably in the descending quality of sound identities established — from exact rhyme in the first stanza to suspended rhyme in the opening of the last stanza, to the complete absence of a sound harmony at the end.

Emily Dickinson's use of disconcerting rhyme variations is the technical manifestation of the sudden oblique light that for her makes all things different. Her light metaphor conveys the experience of momentary and unique insight which is at the heart of her poetic vision. To say that poetry works essentially by indirection, by making familiar words say in combination new things, is to see that poetry is the perfectly appropriate mode of expression for the kind of vision Emily Dickinson possessed. She eventually came to define this vision in poetry and letters of the later years. Through these declarations we may gain understanding of the vision underlying the work of the formative years. This oblique quality of her poetic expression is implicit in "Tell all the Truth but tell it slant" (P–1129):

> Tell all the Truth but tell it slant–
> Success in Circuit lies.

Indirection, too, is the manner in which revelation is said to be achieved:

> There's a certain Slant of light,
> Winter Afternoons–
> That oppresses, like the Heft
> Of Cathedral Tunes–
>
> Heavenly Hurt, it gives us–
> We can find no scar,
> But internal difference,
> Where the Meanings, are.   (P–258)

This imagery compounded from nature and from the church connotes the new and oppressive insight offered in the perception of death (the lifelessness of "Winter Afternoons"). The same symbolic meaning is implicit in a passage from Emily Dickinson's third letter to Higginson (L–265) in the first year of their correspondence: "My dying Tutor told me that he would like to live till I had been a poet, but Death was much of a Mob as I could master — then — And when far afterward — a sudden light on Orchards, or a new fashion in the wind troubled

my attention — I felt a palsy, here — the Verses just relieve." [18]
Conversely, the thought of death may work a strange transformation in her perception. The idea is contained in a passage from a late letter (L–641, dated 1880) to Higginson: "These sudden intimacies with Immortality, are expanse — not Peace — as Lightning at our feet, instills a foreign Landscape." [19] An increased preciseness of vision accompanies heightened states of emotion. She records an experience of this phenomenon in a letter (L–610) to her cousins. She describes the effect of the brilliant light which a neighborhood fire in 1879 created: "So much lighter than day was it, that I saw a caterpillar measure a leaf far down in the orchard." [20] The quality of her poetic vision is similar: intense emotion in the confrontation with lover, with death, or with intimations of immortality provides a unique viewpoint from which more precise perception is possible. The technique of oblique sound patterns reflects this perception and becomes a way of rendering that insight. The uniqueness of the throe of death, for example, is described in the early poem "I like a look of Agony" (P–241). The shocking novelty of the observation is audibly registered in the disparity between sounds at the end of the second and fourth lines:

> The Eyes glaze once–and that is Death–
> Impossible to feign
> The Beads upon the Forehead
> By homely Anguish strung.

The felicitous fusing of the vision and the rhyme technique occurs also in "'Tis so appalling–it exhilirates" (P–281). The sight of death becomes the actual experience of death; this new knowledge of "the worst" is a disquieting experience to which disparate sounds in the closing lines are audible accompaniment:

> 'Tis so appalling–it exhilirates–
> So over Horror, it half Captivates–
> The Soul stares after it, secure–
> To know the worst, leaves no dread more.

In a comic vein, yet in what amounts to a technical tour de force of sound manipulation, Emily Dickinson in the delightful narrative of a robbery, beginning "I know some lonely Houses off the Road" (P–289), describes the approach of dawn and the new light it throws. As the plunderers in the poem are surprised by day, so the reader reacts to the movement of sound as it parallels the oncoming light. The fifth stanza of the poem begins with a vowel rhyme, and then in four subsequent lines the four shifting vowel sounds move with the shifting light. The wit in this verbal game makes in effect a parody of the conventional *aubade*:

> Day–rattles–too
> Stealth's–slow–
> The Sun has got as far
> As the third Sycamore–
> Screams Chanticleer
> "Who's there"?

Emily Dickinson's ingenuity in making sound function in her verse is clearly a significant stylistic feature in the early work. Sound, as she uses it, vitalizes her formal structures and conveys with precise fidelity the vision that impels her poetic expression. Its seemingly wayward cast gives to her verse a powerful show of spontaneity, and readers neither expect nor insist on absolute harmony in the impulsive expressions of the human heart. Those early liberties achieve a fine balance of discordant qualities, which is to say that Emily Dickinson at her best in the early works exercises a control which is the more remarkable because it is sustained against pressures of the greatest emotional intensity.

NEW WAYS OF ARTICULATING
THE WORLD

Out of her impatience with Victorian verbosity and, beyond that, her willful subversion of the stifling reasonableness of language itself, Emily Dickinson refined the authentic speech by which we identify her. An analysis of the disparate elements that contribute to her style will enable us to see the characteristic tendency and wholeness of that style in the formative years and to judge the extent to which it exerted an influence on the mode of her perception. We can see, too, the ways by which she distilled her poetic expression to its irreducible conciseness.

A necessary criterion for judging the level of her achievement in particular works is whether or not the stylistic mannerisms intrude on the argument of the poem and, to the distraction of the reader, dominate the experience the poem attempts to create. One measure, then, is the unobtrusiveness or lucidity (as opposed to opaqueness) of the language. An unsuccessful poem is one in which, to use John Crowe Ransom's term, the texture is so consciously constructed that it is not ultimately irrelevant but rather overpowers the argument of the poem, making the experience of the poem incidental to the rhetorical embellishment. Richard Chase spoke of this weakness in some of the poetry of Emily Dickinson when he referred to her "rococo" manner.[1] The term is useful so far as we take it to mean the manner of treating the ornamental motif as an end in itself. Effectively used, rococo can be a fine, precise expression, admirably concrete, producing the minute delights Wylie Sypher calls "diminished theatre."[2] But where the verbal ornamentation dominates in Emily Dickinson's poetry the compositions are almost always of a lesser poetic success. The suppression of the decorative impulse Chase rightly saw as contributing to the finer style that shapes the best poems: "The motion [Emily Dickinson's] mind takes in passing from her bad poems to her good ones enforces a rigorous subordination of these troublesome images to the whole context of the poem, and sometimes it enforces their total suppression."[3]

Two of the earliest poems are clearly of the ornamental kind. Though certainly neither is intended as a thoroughly serious poetic statement, each displays such verbal dexterity that the interest in these works is almost exclusively confined to the use of language and to the profusion of imagery and analogue. In the valentine beginning "Awake ye muses nine" (P–1), for example, these lines indicate rhetorical versatility:

> The high do seek the lowly, the great do seek the small,
> None cannot find who *seeketh*, on this terrestial ball;
> The bee doth court the flower, the flower his suit receives,
> And they make merry wedding, whose guest are hundred leaves;
> The wind doth woo the branches, the branches they are won,
> And the father fond demandeth the maiden for his son.

The interest here of course is in the profusion of examples of pairings, fitting for a valentine but hardly charged with any profounder intent. In "'Sic transit gloria mundi'" (P–3), the verbal performance glitters less through the imagery than simply in the rush of words. The eleventh stanza, for example, crowds one polysyllabic word upon another:

> Mortality is fatal–
> Gentility is fine,
> Rascality, heroic,
> *Insolvency, sublime!*

Similar to the developmental tendency of certain other poets, of Shakespeare for a particular example, whose *Venus and Adonis* is primarily a display of rhetorical extravagance, Emily Dickinson early in her writing career indulged her linguistic talent sometimes to the exclusion of thematic substance. The early poem "If recollecting were forgetting" (P–33), for example, has interest principally for its playful manipulation of words:

> If recollecting were forgetting,
> Then I remember not.
> And if forgetting, recollecting,
> How near I had forgot.

This manner is not confined to her earliest works; it periodically claimed her talents in the later poetry as well. In the poem "Renunciation–is a piercing Virtue" (P–745), for example, only the solemnity of the argument, the imagery of anguish, and most importantly the insight into the dilemma of renunciation and its great price, save the poem from degenerating into an exercise simply of gratuitous verbal stunts. The flaw is only narrowly avoided in these lines:

> Renunciation–is the Choosing
> Against itself–
> Itself to justify
> Unto itself–
> When larger function–
> Make that appear–
> Smaller–that Covered Vision–Here.

In another late poem, "A nearness to Tremendousness" (P–963), the sentiment (as much as is discernible) cannot assimilate the verbal manipulations adequately for they intrude and arrest the reader's attention. The language becomes a barrier and the poem an exercise in sound rather than in meaning or experience:

> A nearness to Tremendousness–
> An Agony procures–
> Affliction ranges Boundlessness–
> Vicinity to Laws
>
> Contentment's quiet Suburb–
> Affliction cannot stay
> In Acres–It's Location
> Is Illocality.

When, in the early poems, Emily Dickinson effects a deliberate reduction in tone by the use of playful imagery or where the intention for humor or satire or minutely precise imagery is clearly absent, the result seldom rises to genuine poetic achievement. Representative of such stylistic weakness are the poems constructed around the "little boat" and "little people" images. Excerpts from a few of the poems from the early years will illustrate this. The subject of each poem is death, and the apparent occasion is reflection on what lies the other side of death:

> Adrift! A little boat adrift!
> And night is coming down!
> Will *no* one guide a little boat
> Unto the nearest town?   (P–30)

> 'Twas such a little–little boat
> That toddled down the bay!
> 'Twas such a gallant–gallant sea
> That beckoned it away!   (P–107)

> She died–*this* was the way she died.
> And when her breath was done
> Took up her simple wardrobe
> And started for the sun.
> Her little figure at the gate
> The Angels must have spied,
> Since I could never find her
> Upon the mortal side.   (P–150)

Do they wear "new shoes"–in "Eden"–
Is it always pleasant–there–
Wont they scold us–when we're hungry–
Or tell God–how cross we are.

(P–215)

These examples in the rococo manner are to be contrasted
with those instances where Emily Dickinson in writing about
death created the absolutely precise image in which the *drama*
of the particular poem is staged without playful compromise.
Such an example (embodying some of her finest images) is
"How many times these low feet staggered" (P–187):

How many times these low feet staggered–
Only the soldered mouth can tell–
Try–can you stir the awful rivet–
Try–can you lift the hasps of steel!

Stroke the cool forehead–hot so often–
Lift–if you care–the listless hair–
Handle the adamantine fingers
Never a thimble–more–shall wear–

Buzz the dull flies–on the chamber window–
Brave–shines the sun through the freckled pane–
Fearless–the cobweb swings from the ceiling–
Indolent Housewife–in Daisies–lain!

The absolute stasis of death is concretely objectified in the
imagery of metal and stone. The now-vacant mortal habitation
from which the "Housewife" was called is pictured with artful
precision in the flies, the cobweb, and the spotted window pane.
Other examples are to be found in "I like a look of Agony"
(P–241), "I felt a Funeral in my Brain" (P–280), " 'Tis so
appalling–it exhilirates" (P–281), and "A Clock stopped" (P–
287).

Some final examples will demonstrate the sort of unevenness
of Emily Dickinson's achievement in articulating a particular

emotion. In two poems from the early years, in which the subject is the soul's compelling desire for fulfillment, the one has the facile imagery that reduces and distracts. The first stanza of "What shall I do–it whimpers so" (P–186) reads:

> What shall I do–it whimpers so–
> This little Hound within the Heart
> All day and night with bark and start–
> And yet, it will not go–
> Would you *untie* it, were you me–
> Would it stop whining–if to Thee–
> I sent it–even now?

The implied situation of the dog and master is not only trite but, because the tonal quality is indecisive (a failure to bolster the strength of the sentiment for which the image is supposed to work), the effect is compromised and in its own turn diminished from an effective statement. In contrast, in a poem grouped in the following year (1861), the inner impulse is nicely reproduced by the oxymoron "perpetual mention" (with its suggestion of a pun on "perpetual motion") in concert with the imagery of martial dedication and Christ-like commitment. The lines are from "Unto like Story–Trouble has enticed me" (P–295):

> Unto guessed Crests, my moaning fancy, leads me,
> Worn fair
> By Heads rejected–in the lower country–
> Of honors there–
> Such spirit makes her perpetual mention,
> That I–grown bold–
> Step martial–at my Crucifixion–
> As Trumpets–rolled.

The rhetorical maneuver concentrates and maintains the solemn tone of the subject matter. In its connotation of an insistent pulsating force, the expression takes up the image of the chanting prisoners of stanza one, finds its own formal equivalent in the alternating long and short lines (a form unique in the early works), and yokes the contradictory ideas of continuity and brevity. It carries us directly to the meaning, rather than distracting us or impeding our understanding by compromise or cuteness.

Several other elements contribute to the stylistic texture of Emily Dickinson's poetry, and where they succeed they are unobtrusive. They do not contribute, as do the instances of facile rococo, to the imbalance of texture and argument where stylistic devices detract from the poems' effectiveness. Some of these formal elements have already been discussed. Metrical patterns, since they derive from hymnody, contribute their own aspirational tonality. Imagery groupings embody the central perceptual concern of Emily Dickinson with the fundamental disjunction of experience into motion and stasis. Her variations outside conventional rhyme patterns serve to vitalize her formal patterns and to provide auditory correlatives of feeling. Her habitual use of the emphatic opening and closing lines makes a rigid frame for her thoughts and controls the expression which lies between. Another structural device discloses the actual mode of imaginative association by which the poet's mind proceeded. Her tendency is first to establish an equivocal locus of meaning in a poem through imagery that has more than one possible symbolic extension. The poet then proceeds to base her line of thought in only one of the symbolic extensions. The result is that, while the central argument of the poem unfolds, the other symbolic possibilities are held in suspension, functioning as complicating commentary or subdued background texture. In the poem "To learn the Transport by the Pain" (P–167), for example, the principal interpretive problem is to account for the shift in tone from the declamatory statement at the opening,

> To learn the Transport by the Pain–
> As Blind Men learn the sun!

to the desperate tone of resignation of the closing lines in which the chant of exultation of the initiates is

>Inaudible, indeed,
>To us–the duller scholars
>Of the Mysterious Bard!

The apparent shift in tone actually leads to an emphatic affirmation at the end of but one extension of the equivocation established in the first and second stanzas. Lines three and four of the first quatrain represent a major qualification of the assurance of knowledge suggested by the verb "to learn" in the first two lines quoted above:

>To die of thirst–suspecting
>That Brooks in Meadows run!

To *suspect* that there is in some other life a compensation for present anguish represents an order of understanding distinctly different from knowledge possessed. The two viewpoints represented by these two orders of knowledge — the possessed and the suspected — are carried out subtly in the second stanza by way of the ambiguity of "native lands." The second stanza deals most apparently with the sustaining function of the "Laureates," that is, with the duty of instilling faith in those separated from "home":

>To stay the homesick–homesick feet
>Upon a foreign shore–
>Haunted by native lands, the while–
>And blue–beloved air!

Home, however, is equivocal in that it refers both to the final repose in the heavenly home and at the same time to the earthly existence, to the secular home from which one is separated not by death but by geography. The ambiguity of the second stanza — the double value assigned to "home" — reasserts both the religious and the secular orders of knowledge established in the opening stanza. At this point two orders of belief have been posited, the heavenly more strongly than the secular, and the third stanza appears to be an affirmation of the heavenly order of belief, that is, of faith. Those who "believe," who have faith in the ultimate compensation of heaven, are the laureates whose chants (prayers) ascend constantly:

> This is the Sovereign Anguish!
> This–the signal wo!
> These are the patient "Laureates"
> Whose voices–trained–below–
>
> Ascend in ceaseless Carol.

The title "Laureate" is also ambiguous, referring both to those crowned by God's grace and to the poets whose crown is a different order of immortality. That the word "Laureates" is enclosed in quotation marks helps indicate that the title is transferable, that it is applicable to both the heavenly and secular conditions. Now the closing three lines of the poem, which seemed a distinct shift in tone from affirmation to skepticism, have a clear relationship and genesis in the undertone of secularism and skepticism suggested earlier by the qualifying verb "suspect," by the equivocal denotation of "native land," and by the two orders of "Laureates." The poet has throughout the poem been committed to the secular view. Out of the ambiguous thematic locus of faith the poet has all the while been pursuing the extension that is faith-less. The ending declares, therefore, that the prayers of those who believe they are saved are inaudible, and consequently have no meaning for those others, the speaker included, who, being the dull scholars of God ("the Mysterious Bard"), are left only with the secular implications previously established: they are left only with suspicion of a heaven, only with the native land on which they stand, and only with the type of crown that is available to those rejected of heaven. The sounds of faith, then, are

> Inaudible, indeed,
> To us–the duller scholars
> Of the Mysterious Bard!

The progression of the thought and tonality has been concerned only with one of the equivocal positions established in the first three stanzas. The poet's mind is directed only to the skeptical undertones, while playing off against them in counterpoint of tone the exultation of assured belief in salvation. Other poems have a similar pattern, and the subjective manner of thought association is most often revealed, as in the poem above, by an apparent shift in tone or commitment. The poem beginning "If I could bribe them by a rose" (P–179) is another example from the early works, as is "'Tis so appalling–it exhilirates" (P–281). This structural element of Emily Dickinson's style is seen to be in certain poems related less directly to conscious thought progression than to tonal values, which in turn represent not the rational working out of an argument but rather an elusive design imposed by the emotions.

Emily Dickinson's poetic vocabulary has been characterized in several and sometimes contradictory ways. The reason for disagreement is that subjective interpretations (as indicated earlier, often the *only* manner of interpretation possible for poems that encourage free inference) tend to ascribe more importance to certain recurring words than to others. The result is that assertions concerning Emily Dickinson's vocabulary are sometimes based simply upon impressionistic responses. For example, Henry Wells tells us that the poet employs a "large vocabulary including many rare words and some of her own manufacture," [4] while R. P. Blackmur describes her store of diction as "a small, rigidly compartmented vocabulary of general and conventional groups of terms, plus a moderately capacious vocabulary of homely, acute, directly felt words from which the whole actualizing strength of her verse is drawn." [5] In fact, as shown most convincingly by William Howard, the vocabulary of Emily Dickinson is in only a few respects different from that of other poets writing in English. [6] Her words are drawn from as wide a variety of experience as other important poets have turned to, and include expressions both concrete and abstract, formal and colloquial, latinate and Anglo-Saxon, technical and common, literal and figurative. The brevity of her verses, I submit, however, in most instances places a greater burden upon individual words for meaning than is the case in more expansive verse. Often for Emily Dickinson a single word must carry *all* of the meaning without the benefit of contextual help from additional and qualifying words.

Richard Chase declares that "a major technical flaw in Emily Dickinson's poetry is the lack of perspicuity in her abstract words." [7] I do not believe he means that her words have any less denotative precision than they normally possess but rather that they appear without expansive qualification and contextual definition. Essentially this is a problem related to the magnitude of her individual poetic utterances (a problem discussed below). John Crowe Ransom judges that much of her verse locates itself around key abstract words, which in turn represent "a special Americanism" quite in consonance with a typical national political feeling which has turned on such abstract expressions as *Democracy* and *Equality*. Blackmur's and Ransom's views, however, are impressionistic judgments, and are not borne out by Howard's study, which conclusively shows that "her poetic vocabulary is reasonably large and certainly inclusive, but it is not repetitious. Nor is it particularly unconventional or original." [8] Indeed, the study shows that a problematical word such as *Circumference*, for example, appears only sixteen times in the 19,100 lines of poetry in the Johnson edition. In addition, of the list of seventeen words of highest frequency (occurring eight or more times per thousand lines) in the Dickinson vocabulary, no single word is in the least unconventional. [9] Howard's conclusion regarding Emily Dickinson's genuine originality in diction is interesting particularly for its disclosure of the high ratio of verbs she uses. This finding supports my own contention that central to her perception are the phenomena of motion and rest, states denoted most directly by verbs. Other unique uses of language by the poet do not appear in Howard's conclusion, so that her whole originality is not fully indicated merely by statistical word counts. Howard does, however, indicate rightly that it is not the vocabulary itself but rather the way in which the poet puts words together that is most uniquely the core of her style. He concludes that

> it is not [in] the words she uses but the way in which she uses them that Emily Dickinson is most original. Three idiosyncrasies are apparent: her ratio of 5:12:8 for adjectives, nouns, and verbs [as compared to the average ratio 9:17:10 for the one hundred poets in Josephine Miles's study, *The Continuity of Poetic Language* (Berkeley, 1951)]; the small number of words — only 17 — that she uses 8 or more times per 1,000 lines; and her occasional use of many words in a somewhat singular way, e.g., the use of a noun to denote a quality possessed by the thing for which the noun stands.[10]

Certain of these singular usages warrant discussion for they are persistent elements which contribute to the early Dickinson style and, perhaps more than anything else in her poetry, give it its identifiable uniqueness. Her effort bent toward particularization rather than the reverse of generalizing from an initial precise perception. To express her vision with finality she was compelled not to make her own minute feelings reveal a general truth for others, but rather to take what others had also seen and felt and expressed (in the hymn, for example) and refine that to suit her own purposes. It was this constant effort toward particularizing what the received form could communicate that prompted her experimentation in unique forms of expression.

The first of these elements, and one that has received direct critical attention, is her use of what has been called the subjunctive mood. In certain early poems, the usage is indeed the subjunctive:

> I pray him too–explore
> The Lark's pure territory.   (P–15)

> We should not mind so small a flower–
> Except it quiet bring
> Our little garden that we lost
> Back to the Lawn again.   (P–81)

> Grant God, he charge the bravest
> Of all the martial blest!   (P–147)

> Teach me the skill,

> That I instil the pain.   (P–177)

Current disuse of this verb form explains perhaps its impact on contemporary readers and the attention it has drawn in critical responses to the poetry.[11] It seems to appear gratuitously in other places in Emily Dickinson's work, but there it is not subjunctive form; rather it is an eccentric usage without sanction in conventional grammar. Once again the later poems help define the interpretive problem we find in the work of the early years. For example, in the fine poem beginning "Further in Summer than the Birds" (P–1068), seven lines in the third and fourth stanzas, describing the Mass-like quality of the cricket's hum, read:

> When August burning low
> Arise this spectral Canticle
> Repose to typify
>
> Remit as yet no Grace
> No Furrow on the Glow
> Yet a Druidic Difference
> Enhances Nature now.

The late-summer crickets, in their ritualistic chanting, bear witness to the spiritual repose attendant upon a salvation which is not yet certain, not yet "remitted," but only indicated: when August nears its end, this ghostly song evokes a vision of heaven, yet remits no certainty of Grace. Richard Chase interprets this usage as a device to suggest what is volitive, optative, potential.[12] But this characterization is not completely satisfactory for it still associates the usage with the conventional subjunctive mood. Whicher's reasoning is less helpful, suggesting that the form (not quite clearly) indicates fear and uneasiness: "The tension of her poetry seems to have thrown her into a state of chronic trepidation which only the subjunctive could express." [13] Thomas Johnson believes that this usage represents an attempt through verbal device to give her meanings a general timeless application. "She was trying," he says, "to universalize her thought to embrace past, present, and future." [14] The most plausible reasoning is provided by Charles Anderson. In discussing the poem beginning "Essential Oils–are wrung" (P–675), he refers to the final stanza of this two-stanza poem:

> The General Rose decay–
> While this–in Lady's Drawer
> Make Summer, when the Lady lie
> In Spiceless Sepulchre.[15]

Of the verb forms in these lines, Anderson concludes:

Perhaps it was her desire to emphasize the absolute truth of what she was saying that led her to the puzzling verb forms employed here, 'decay,' 'make,' 'lie.' Her usage is certainly idiosyncratic, but one may conjecture a purpose that fits with the general intention of this poem. By omitting the final s she was trying to get down to the basic stem of the verbs, their pure uninflected verbal quality, paring away number, mood, and even the partial limitation in time implied by the present tense. By this ruse she was seeking to escape from all particularity — of quantity, quality, even calendar — into the Absolute: rose decay, just as poet die, but perfume make summer.[16]

This is persuasive reasoning and embodies the interpretations of both Chase and Johnson. I should add to this, however, what seems to me to be an inescapable quality of her use of this unconventional verb form. In both "Further in Summer than the Birds" and "Essential Oils–are wrung" the tone is incantatory, and the meanings chanted are general declaratory meanings, general truths, intended to be affective, and attesting to the mystical quality of essential oils (poetry) and of the crickets' incantatory humming. Indeed, the final declaration of "Further in Summer than the Birds" seems unmistakable evidence of the ritualistic intention: "a Druidic Difference / Enhances Nature now."

In an early poem, the gnomic quality is evident but lacks the incantatory tonality. The poem "A *Wounded* Deer–leaps highest" (P–165) includes these lines beginning the final quatrain:

> Mirth is the Mail of Anguish–
> In which it Cautious Arm.

She seems on other occasions to be attempting a verbal, and indeed visual (for the inflections are visibly pared away), correlative for the insight into *essences* at the core of meaning and experience. This technique is not confined to verb forms alone. In the poem "I have never seen 'Volcanoes'" (P–175), she has trimmed the *s* off *guns* to suggest the essential quality, here the explosive quality, of ordnance.

> I have never seen 'Volcanoes'–
> But, when Travellers tell
> How those old–phlegmatic mountains
> Usually so still–
>
> Bear within–appalling Ordnance,
> Fire, and smoke, and gun,
> Taking Villages for breakfast,
> And appalling Men.

Grammatical constrictions give way to the desire to get at quality rather than objective appearances. The device represents Emily Dickinson's attempt to grasp the *feeling* which objects or events evoke rather than the mere experience of sensuous perception.

Prodigal capitalization is another point of style in her early poetry. Little discernible consistency marks her use of capitals; it seems to be diffuse and indiscriminate, certain critical assertions on the matter notwithstanding. Higginson believed the habit to be no more than a vestige of customary usage in related languages. He refers to Emily Dickinson's "habit as to capitalization, as the printers call it, in which she followed the Old English and present German method of thus distinguishing every noun substantive." [17] Emily Dickinson does not of course make a consistent practice of capitalizing every noun substantive. However, Higginson's attempt to derive the poet's mannerism historically suggests indirectly a general practice on her part of distinguishing *visually* her pivotal words, those both precise and abstract, about which the idea of the poem revolves. Another effect of the poet's persistent capitalization is suggested by Ransom when he terms this mannerism "a mythopoeic device, to push [the words] a little further into the fertile domain of myth." [18]

Ransom's purpose certainly is not to suggest that Emily Dickinson relies upon allusion to a definite body of myth to focus her meanings. In most cases, whatever mythic quality emerges in her poetry stems from a personal mythology, more often than not imprecise and suggestive, generating free implications rather than congealing meaning. We must recognize, of course, that no single explanation serves to define the specific effect Emily Dickinson intended or achieved by her habit of capitalization; rather, we may conclude that the usage is diffuse, indiscriminate, and in different poems serves to produce different effects. Certain generalizations may be made, however, about her capitalization, and though not consistent in application to specific poems always, the generalizations indicate ways in which her poetic imagination operates. First of all, the habit of capitalization often distills from the individual work those strongly operative words which carry the burden of the imagery and meaning and which, consequently, form the framework of the poem. The first quatrain of "There's a certain Slant of light" (P–258) illustrates this quality of distillation:

> There's a certain Slant of light,
> Winter Afternoons–
> That oppresses, like the Heft
> Of Cathedral Tunes.

The capitalized words here (excluding the insignificant initial words) — *Slant, Winter Afternoons, Heft,* and *Cathedral Tunes* — are focal supports; they carry the argument, which is then refined by the words *certain* (to distinguish the special quality of light) and *oppresses* (which embodies the quality of the emotional reaction to the experience here recreated). *Slant* fixes the visual image, as does *Winter Afternoons,* which evokes the bodily and emotional reactions to the setting and time of year (a time of emotional cold, despair, fear, isolation). The remaining three capitalized words combine to form the simile, which defines more precisely the emotional reaction to the experience of the revelatory power of nature in special instances. The six capitalized words do the main job of communication and dramatic service in this first quatrain, providing the perceptual experience, the setting, both seasonal and emotional, and reinforcing the image with the precise simile "like the *Heft* / Of *Cathedral Tunes.*"

But to say that the manner of capitalization is confined to distinguishing the focal words is to isolate only a part of the function of this device. For beyond the essential meanings and images which these words convey there are radiated additional and rich connotative qualities. These words, by being visually distinguished, indicate that their normal meanings have been enriched in the poem with added intent. They are charged, so to speak, and are to be interpreted with heightened sensitivity. *Winter Afternoons* denotes not only the scene but the entire range of sensuous reactions (cold, inactivity, whiteness) and emotional response (apprehension, meditation, isolation). The full drama of the senses and the emotions is aroused in gathering together the possible connotative values of these words which have been distinguished by being capitalized. *Heft* is similarly rich with connotation, for it speaks to the tactile sense and reinforces the verb *oppresses*, and, in its most artful extension, arouses in combination with *Cathedral Tunes* the feeling of thorough vibrancy — a sort of sympathetic vibration of the senses — evoked by the heavy and palpable thrumming of the organ chords. These distinguished words enrich the texture of the poem by inducing free and prolific associations which provide the context for its meaning.

On occasion, this habit of capitalization can be forcefully effective, for it first distills the essential words (both of meaning and imagery), it distinguishes them and consequently indicates that they are charged with a meaning and sentiment which, by activating the reader's own remembrance of perceptual and emotional experiences, engage him thoroughly and induce the free and personal associations which in turn activate the words themselves.[19] The effect is reciprocal, for as the distinguished words activate the sensitivities and experiential reservoir of the reader, the connotative quality of the words is in turn intensified. The cycle of meaning, of evocation and reaction, is then self-generating, and the contextual implications from this minimal verbal stimulus are built up and combined and recombined until the words are operating at heightened force. The ultimate result is the highest achievement of lyrical poetry. The poem ceases to be an external object of contemplation and becomes in fact experience, recreating within the reader a semblance of the experience itself and not merely an inert reference to it.[20]

Emily Dickinson's use of the dash, like the capital, in many instances is indiscriminate and without particular significance. Yet, the dash operates sometimes in a way similar to the capital, for it serves to distinguish words, to isolate them for the eye and, in turn, for the interpretive faculties of the reader. The device was a common one in hymnody, and its use there suggests the meanings Emily Dickinson occasionally attached to this form of punctuation. In the preface to Watts's *Psalms, Hymns and Spiritual Songs*, for example, the editor, the Reverend Mr. Samuel Worcester, declares: "In the *punctuation* regard has been had to musical expression. In some instances, therefore, different points or pauses are inserted, from what would have been used, had the grammatical construction, only, been regarded. The *dash* is intended to denote an expressive suspension. In order to good expression, a distinct and judicious observance of the pauses is absolutely necessary." [21] This is not to insist that Emily Dickinson deliberately derived her use of the dash from hymnody or that she is consistent enough in its usage in the early work to justify arguing a specific function for it in the poems. Rather, her use of the dash, like her use of capitalization, serves on occasion as a visual distinguishing mark, an admonition to the reader to allow every word so set apart its full measure of interpretation. The function, like that of the capital letters, is *indicative*. Like her use of exact rhyme as a sensitizing device, the dash sensitizes the reader's reactions, activates the responsive reservoirs of the reader, ultimately standing as a graphic representation in the poem of the presence of the creative impulse, of the *spontaneity* of the emotional force that went into the composition. It indicates, therefore, the emotional force that is to be derived from the poem. That Emily Dickinson used the device often and used it indiscriminately in some cases, of course, weakens its impact upon the reader. The dash becomes a familiar and therefore sometimes an ineffective device. But used decisively, it serves to announce that the poem is "haunted," to use the poet's own term, that it has lurking qualities for the searching reader.[22] Where it is successful, it artfully impedes the ease of reading, forcing, at first only visually but then mentally, a savoring of the words and expressions thus isolated and distinguished.

The poem "A little Bread–a crust–a crumb" (P–159) will indicate the effective use of the dash:

> A little Bread–a crust–a crumb–
> A little trust–a demijohn–
> Can keep the soul alive–
> Not portly, mind! but breathing–warm–
> Conscious–as old Napoleon,
> The night before the Crown!
>
> A modest lot–A fame petite–
> A brief Campaign of sting and sweet
> Is plenty! Is enough!
> A *Sailor's* business is *the shore!*
> A *Soldier's–balls!* Who asketh more,
> Must seek the neighboring life!

The argument here is that even though the achievement of "A fame petite" is as much as this life affords, preservation of the soul (both spiritual and poetic) is absolutely necessary for sustaining one in the "brief Campaign" of preparation for immortality (the "neighboring life"). This double sense of the smallness of inspiration ("A little Bread") and the importance of it to sustain one for whom the grander life is remote, is efficiently conveyed by the use of the dash. In the lines quoted, the dash isolates the metaphorical equivalents of minimal inspiration. It emphasizes their smallness, the fragmentary nature of the sustaining "food." The repetition, on the other hand, as effectively suggests the crucial importance of this small sustenance. The dash, by creating a formal visual image of fragmentation and insistence, signals the paradox. A similar emphasis occurs, for example, in "I'm 'wife'–I've finished that" (P–199), and "If *He* dissolve–then–there is *nothing–more*" (P–236).

Like her capitalization, of course, the employment of the dash is only one of several devices, one technical operation to enrich the texture of the poem. It contributes to the wholeness of Emily Dickinson's style, but must necessarily be seen in relation to other devices. In isolation, as here for purposes of discussion, it seems to take on an unjustified importance. However, it should not be dismissed merely as an expendable mannerism in her poetry. For to remove the dash completely, as Johnson recommends, would be to deny the poems the illusion of spontaneity and intimacy it provides.[23] To delete the dash where it *seems* to be ineffective, on the other hand, is to impose a reading on the poems, allowing the poet her habit in regard to certain expressions while denying her this intention in other instances.

A number of other devices also contribute to the rich stylistic texture and wholeness of Emily Dickinson's early poetic art. Some of these contrivances have been referred to as word tricks.[24] Among them are the recurrent habits of disorienting the reader's expectations by substituting an abstract word for an expected concrete word (and vice versa), by employing a noun to denote the quality of the object rather than its image, and by synesthetic employment of imagery. This disconcertion of the reader's expectations, in a manner not unlike that by which music proceeds, expands contextual possibilities, increases the reader's awareness, and deepens the emotional experience the poems recreate. Some representative examples of her word-play will illustrate. In the early poem beginning "The feet of people walking home" (P–7), the final stanza of eight lines is a simple affirmation of a private faith in immortality (literary or spiritual or both), a faith that exists as a consequence of a private revelation. The final three lines of the stanza declare:

> My faith that Dark adores–
> Which from it's solemn abbeys
> Such resurrection pours.

Dark is the metaphorical rendition of the inscrutability of the future; the argument is that faith exists in spite of and even

because of the not knowing. Dark antecedes the *solemn abbeys,*
and the poet, continuing the religious metaphor into the last
line, employs the appropriate image of organ music pouring
forth from the chapels. Yet Emily Dickinson gives this music a
conceptual meaning by substituting the abstraction *resurrection*
for the normally expected and more concrete *music.* In other
words, the substitution of the idea for the precise sensuous experience concisely combines the percept and the concept. The
device functions here to expand and deepen the meaning. The
denial of the reader's expectations operates to compel a more
affective reading as it provokes the mind's effort to reconcile the
expected image with what actually appears in the poem.

We find the technique in the poem "I felt a Funeral, in my
Brain" (P–280). The third and fourth stanzas recreate the horror of total and rapt attention to one's own despair, as if no other
reality existed. The totality of the sensation is the ultimate
measure of the desperation:

> And then I heard them lift a Box
> And creak across my Soul
> With those same Boots of Lead, again,
> Then Space–began to toll,
>
> As all the Heavens were a Bell,
> And Being, but an Ear,
> And I, and Silence, some strange Race
> Wrecked, solitary, here.

The word trick (at base, the metaphorical equation) in these
lines is the substitution of the abstraction *Space* for the normally
anticipated *bells,* which is clearly implied by the verb *to toll.*
The poet's purpose here, again, is to employ the reasonable
supposition of bells in the reader's mind, and then by the substitution to give this image meaning, the meaning here being the
sense of utter emptiness brought on by grief and by the consequent breakdown of rational thought. The speaker is saying

that it is the sensation of emptiness which, paradoxically like tolling bells, vibrates throughout the being and destroys the silence one normally associates with emptiness. Despair becomes both *understood* (as destructive) and *felt* (as the tolling of the death knell). In fusing understanding and feeling, the poem demonstrates here that quality of poetic vision we have come to call unified sensibility.

In other early poems she reverses the substitution, placing a specific image in the syntax where an abstraction is anticipated. The device is of course a form of metaphor and a method of embodying conceptual understanding. The poet makes the identification explicit, for example, in "I've known a Heaven, like a Tent" (P–243), and in "'Hope' is the thing with feathers" (P–254). In "Besides the Autumn poets sing" (P–131) the abstraction of winter is rejected for the precise and concrete image of *snow*, and the midsummer season becomes simply *haze*.

> Besides the Autumn poets sing
> A few prosaic days
> A little this side of the snow
> And that side of the Haze.

Time here, the passing of the seasons, is not only established conceptually by the normally expected words, but it is made imaginatively concrete by the synecdochic figures of snow and haze. The poet refers here to the transitional days that evade the autumnal clichés of conventional poetic treatment — to the days that are neither summer, fall, nor winter, and to those contemplative days in a person's late life when death occupies thought.

Another early technique, more novel and more striking, which contributes to the totality of Emily Dickinson's style in the formative period is her manner of using a substantive noun to suggest not the object itself but the quality inherent in that object. The device appears early in her career in "As if some little Arctic flower" (P–180), where the poet speaks of "firmaments of sun."

Sun here is used not literally, but rather to convey metaphorically a sky with the qualities of the sun, that is, blazing color, brightness, and warmth. In "If pain for peace prepares" (P–63), she speaks of the bright repose of immortality following the dark despair of this life:

> If night stands first–*then* noon
> To gird us for the sun,
> What gaze!

The effect of *gaze!* here is not limited to the visual image of concentration although that meaning is embodied. The word is employed also for its emotional connotation, the feeling of rapt attention, the highly charged quality of the act of gazing. A similar transfer from object to the feeling evoked is apparent also in "I've known a Heaven, like a Tent" in the expression "miles of Stare." The connotation of the quality of the action that the noun represents operates to make the image compactly expressive.

In the early work as well Emily Dickinson substitutes words denoting emotional states for expected abstractions, as, for example, in "Where I have lost, I softer tread" (P–104), in the closing stanza:

> Why, I have lost, the people know
> Who dressed in frocks of purest snow
> Went home a century ago
> Next Bliss!

Bliss conveys the emotional quality of rapture arising from the thought of resurrection, the achievement of grace, and the consequent understanding of the meaning of life and death. The phrase "a century ago / Next Bliss!" relies for its meaning on the familiar colloquial expression we would use to measure a century already begun and to be terminated in the future. Emily Dickinson distills the immensity of the thought of death and resurrection into that homely phrase. In "Our lives are Swiss" (P–80), she establishes a geographical analogue for life, continuing the figure in the analogue for death (the Alps) and resurrection (Italy). At the same time she relies on the stereotype notion of the placid Swiss to communicate the idea of emotional composure on the craggy peaks of emotional distress. Her habit of relying for effect on stereotype reaction is also readily apparent in her repeated use of foreign names — Bosporus, Cashmere, Vevey, Tunis. These various metaphorical techniques complicate the texture of her poems, for the reader, already in possession of the normally expected words, suddenly confronts new dimensions which combine with the expected to compound expressiveness. Yet formally, we must recognize again, she maintains the almost absolute concision which is a mark of her poetry.

Still another contrivance enhancing the texture of her work is the synesthetic image. The device gives a special edge in "A Route of Evanescence" (P–1463) to the line "A Resonance of Emerald." The fusion occurs between the auditory denotation of *resonance* and the visual reference of the color *Emerald*. The hummingbird seems to be seen and heard simultaneously through the suggestion in the diction of the power of color to be felt. The device appears in her poetry as early as 1859 in the poem "These are the days when Birds come back" (P–130). Indian summer she refers to as "A blue and gold mistake."

> These are the days when Birds come back–
> A very few–a Bird or two–
> To take a backward look.
>
> These are the days when skies resume
> The old–old sophistries of June–
> A blue and gold mistake.

The synthesis joins the logical concept of error with the colors in which this error is manifested, that is, in the summer-like days of late Autumn. In "Musicians wrestle everywhere" (P–157), she writes of the cosmic music of revelation, a "silver strife" without discernible origin.

> Musicians wrestle everywhere–
> All day–among the crowded air
> I hear the silver strife–
> And–waking–long before the morn–
> Such transport breaks upon the town
> I think it that "New life"!

The word *strife* is sufficiently oblique in reference to music that it connotes also the spiritual turmoil such revelation evokes. To describe the strife by an adjective of color and of material value is again to charge the concise phrase with a synthesis of feeling and understanding. Her phrase, referred to earlier, "the Heft / Of Cathedral Tunes" is likewise a synthesis of sensory responses.

On occasion in the early poetry Emily Dickinson uses parts of speech in novel ways, making nouns function as adjectives, adjectives as nouns, and nouns as adverbs. The result is again to fuse word functions, providing in the single word both the image and the feeling to be evoked. She writes of "Cobweb attitudes" (P–105), for example, where the noun serves as adjective. She makes nouns serve as adverbs in expressions such as "Britain born," "Cuckoo born," and "Orchard sprung" (P–285). In her manipulation of normal diction she also makes collective nouns denote singular and specific objects, as when she writes of "a music" (P–14) and "a blood" (P–77).

> She did not sing as we did–
> It was a different tune–
> Herself to her a music
> As Bumble bee of June.

> I never hear the word "escape"
> Without a quicker blood,
> A sudden expectation,
> A flying attitude!

On the other hand, she sometimes makes the specific object function as a collective noun, as in the poem "I have never seen

'Volcanoes'" (P–175), where she writes of "phlegmatic moun-tains" (and means, too, the emotions in turmoil) which

> Bear within–appalling Ordnance,
> Fire, and smoke, and gun.

Gun, used in conjunction with the collective nouns *Fire* and *smoke*, becomes in its turn a collective noun, suggesting, as we have seen, the general *quality* of guns. This technical device functions well enough as a universalizing agent, for it allows the poet to have in a single expression both the general sense and the specific instance of the general.

Punning is still another characteristic technique of Emily Dickinson's style in her early work. The instances of punning in the poem "Some things that fly there be" (P–89) have already been discussed. In another poem (P–27), she describes a dead girl as being "mute from transport."

> Morns like these–we parted–
> Noons like these–she rose–
> Fluttering first–then firmer
> To her fair repose.

> Never did she lisp it–
> It was not for me–
> She–was mute from transport–
> I–from agony.

Transport conveys both physical and emotional qualities, the taking away in death and the rapturous transport of achieving spiritual immortality. In "I shall keep singing!" (P–250), as a poet speaking about her hope of immortality through literary accomplishment, she refers to other lesser poets, "Each–with a Robin's expectation," and then of her own "Redbreast," a word which associates her generically with the other poets but indi-cates also the anguish from which her poetic expression erupts.

Similar ambiguity appears in the last line of the third stanza of the well-known poem "One dignity delays for all" (P–98).

She is speaking of the pomp that attends even the lowliest at his public funeral. The ambiguity resides in the word *raise*:

> What dignified Attendants!
> What service when we pause!
> How loyally at parting
> Their hundred hats they raise!

The lifted hats depict both the solemnity of the occasion when the people stand bareheaded about the open grave and the aura of celebration at a coronation when the gesture signifies joy. The image reaches into the core of the poem's meaning: death's public observance is a strange ceremony, at once solemn and fearful, colorful and grotesquely gay. This single figure, in a way we have now come to expect in Emily Dickinson's style, boldly yokes widely divergent, even contradictory, emotions.

Her habit of personification is too well known to warrant detailed discussion here. Along with the concision of her expression, as it is shaped by both form and device (truncated verb forms, capitalization, dash, substitution, shifting grammatical categories, the pun), the repeated use early in her career of the technique of personification is a major mark of her poetic style. Here are representative examples:

> There is a word
> Which bears a sword   (P–8)

> The wolf came peering curious–
> The owl looked puzzled down–   (P–9)

> The morns are meeker than they were–   (P–12)

> Some Rainbow–coming from the Fair!   (P–64)

> A Lady white, within the Field
> In placid Lily sleeps!   (P–74)

Where this figurative device is most successful it vitalizes concepts, giving them a familiar and readily accessible embodiment. It serves, in other words, to join idea and emotion, the senses and the understanding.

The artistry to which this broad range of stylistic devices contributes in the early poetry of Emily Dickinson may be usefully summarized in its three major characteristics. The first is her artful generation of multiple contexts, the placing of meaning at several levels of experience. This complex creation is more than simply a duality of meaning; there is a multiplicity beyond mere analogue which characterizes her early work. As we have seen, the path of fulfillment for this poet in many instances lies in a fusing of the quest for love, for literary immortality, and for spiritual salvation. The quest takes place in the knowledge that gain must forever entail loss. Her personae search for love at the same time it is renounced, for literary recognition at the same time that recognition is avoided, and for salvation at the same time that faith is rejected. Richard Chase sees in the poetic expression of this quest a simple duality: "Tension in Emily Dickinson is a relationship of the rococo and the sublime. Most every poem exhibits both orders of experience." [25] His description recognizes that Emily Dickinson's poetry operates on both the level of the concrete and the universal. We see, however, that the so-called doubleness is more often a multiplicity of statement. Her style is allusive in its imagery, ambiguous in its symbolism, and, because it is indicative (without clear contextual basis), open to broad inference on the part of the reader. The poems, this is to say, create a precise sentiment for which the reader is often free to supply a variety of experiential contexts. Paradoxically, and by great artistry, she accomplishes this multiplicity with almost irreducible concision.

The second major accomplishment of Emily Dickinson's early stylistic manner is her ability to bring the formless remembrance of experience into intense and present reality. The minute objectifying is particularly acute, for example, in "I felt a Funeral in my Brain" (P–280). Bereavement and despair and the subsequent loss of rational powers are staged in the private theater of the mind. That poem is the ultimate working out of the insight the poet attempted earlier in the poem beginning "It did not surprise me" (P–39). The sentiment here also registers loss:

> This was but a Birdling–
> What and if it be
> One within my bosom
> Had departed me?
>
> This was but a story–
> What and if indeed
> There were just such coffin
> In the heart instead?

This last image finds exact expression in "I felt a Funeral in my Brain." The artistry is in the elaborate drama and movement — the moving to and fro, the restlessness of the mourners (and the emotions) — culminating in the final destructive moment when "a Plank in Reason, broke."

The third principal characteristic of Emily Dickinson's early style is, of course, its concision. Her frugality on occasion is so rigorous as to prevent really meaningful communication. Yet the concision becomes achieved artistry when the very meagerness of the expression is capable of evoking extended and intricate auras of sense and context. There is a paradoxical formal spareness yet connotative richness of statement in her poetry. In an early poem (P–87), she attempted to compress the experience of death, the funeral, and the ensuing grief into the seven words of the opening line:

> A darting fear–a pomp–a tear.

The experience of accustoming oneself to the loss and to the new knowledge that death is both irreparable and at the same time somewhat reassuring because the departed is in heaven, informs the three brief lines which close the quatrain:

> A waking on a morn
> to find that what one waked for,
> inhales the different dawn.

This sort of frugality has an earnestness and latent power about it which a more extended treatment would dissipate. There is an essentiality in the concise style of Emily Dickinson that is remarkably effective. She was capable of distilling emotional turmoil into its essence to the point where feeling exists dissociated from the outer world. The poems become experience rather than mirrors of experience, attesting to the mature artistry Emily Dickinson had achieved in the early years, artistry of such a high order that not even its possessor's mask of diffidence could obscure it.

THE EARLY ACHIEVEMENT

We can be sure that the essential body of Emily Dickinson's fully realized poetic expression will grow as the canon receives renewed critical attention. Her occasional pieces of undistinguished intent and her periodic reversions to adolescent versifying will recede to the periphery of her art, and we shall rediscover those neglected but brilliant pools in which are distilled her bold experimentation and her mature artistry. Many are to be found here in the work of the early years when Emily Dickinson repeatedly realized the furthest extent of her artistic capabilities. Eminent critics have remarked on a few of these early poems, but we recognize now that in more than two dozen prior to the flood years of 1862 and after, she had mined the richest depths of her creative resources.[1] In these works we discern the distinctive qualities of her creative mind: an audaciousness born of irrepressible candor, a startling sensitivity that was yet sufficiently controlled to be refracted through the instrument of irony and wit, a tragic understanding not to be compromised by the promise of heaven or the onslaught of despair, a latent nervous energy the more remarkable for its disciplined release. We discern, too, the distinctive qualities of her art: its bold disregard of conventional shapeliness, the surprise of its novel verbal strategies, its seizure of the significant image, its disconcerting integrity in psychological disclosures, its firm control of powerful emotion.

Like filings in a magnetic field, those early poems which assert her genius define the emotional contours of the central theme of aspiration. In them she savors the distance between desire and its goal. Where specific poems have a dramatic immediacy as performance, the speaker, in one or the other attitude of her divergent roles or in an attitude constituted of both, is distinct and impressive. In several of these compositions of highest achievement, the metrical base provides occasion for the irony, and the central metaphorical construct of motion and stasis orders the perceptions. Throughout, instances of rhyme variation and stylistic mannerism that we now recognize as Emily Dickinson's unique mode of expression charge the poems with urgency, create the feelings of spontaneity and sincerity, and make us constantly aware of the immanence of the creative personality.

In diverse ways, each element contributes to the concision and accompanying complexity of her expression, and ultimately to that fine interior control she exercises over the emotional vitality within her poems. Indeed, in her finest poems the emotional experience reaches an intensity that necessarily reveals at the same time the stylistic control which prevents those feelings from lapsing into intemperance. Her success in confining the centrifugal pressures of emotions within an aesthetic framework represents perhaps her highest achievement as an artist. That achievement of control which would not stifle the intensity she intended to express undoubtedly posed her most challenging problem. The questing condition and the recurrent recognition that mortality forever denies ideal fulfillment are states inherently subject to the extremes of emotion. Yet, even though for Emily Dickinson the emotions mediated her experience, her art allowed her to order those potentially destructive psychic responses.

The principal method by which she resolved this problem of control is her absolute distillation of expression, which provides not only a formal control but so closely circumscribes emotions that they cannot trail off into self-indulgence. This ability of extreme condensation attests also to her powers of psychological insight, for with the greatest economy of terms she could reach directly to the core of a particular feeling. This habit of the elliptic expression, however, sometimes fragments her compositions. The early works provide numerous examples of the precise and piercing expression, yet these fragments of genius sometimes constitute the single effective element of otherwise unsuccessful poems. Foreshadowings of her consummate artistry reside in these brilliant expressions which typify her poetic mode.

A complete gathering of her markedly felicitous and distinctly Dickinsonion phrases would be an extensive one, for early in her career the ability to compact articulation in deceptively simple terms is fully developed. Among her reflections on death, for example, she distills in two lines the recognition of the inevitability of death:

> Good night, because we must,
> How intricate the dust!   (P-114)

In rebellious pose, she concentrates in political metaphor the recognition of the uncommitted state of her soul, declaring that

> Imps in eager Caucus
> Raffle for my Soul!   (P-139)

She imaginatively constructs in homely metaphor the experience of death in the absence of any guiding faith:

> Dying! Dying in the night!
> Wont somebody bring the light
> So I can see which way to go
> Into the everlasting snow?   (P-158)

Early, too, she was capable of pressing her reflections on the precise moment of death into remarkably concise expressions. She seems repeatedly to have applied herself to formulating an answer to the problem posed in the line which begins an otherwise unsuccessful poem: "She died–*this* was the way she died"

(P–150). Fixing upon the image of the open eyes glazed in death, she defines that condition as

> . . . but our rapt attention
> To Immortality.   (P–7)

She precisely objectifies the abstract terms by picturing the final physical convulsion:

> A throe upon the features–
> A hurry in the breath–
> An extasy of parting
> Denominated "Death."   (P–71)

The qualities of utter finality and motionlessness she describes succinctly as

> The quiet nonchalance of death–
> No Daybreak–can bestir.   (P–194)

Defined irreverently in the terms of commerce, death is

> . . . just the price of *Breath*–
> With but the "Discount" of the *Grave*–
> Termed by the *Brokers–"Death"*!   (P–234)

Death personified is a frighteningly efficient workman. He is:

> Industrious! Laconic!
> Punctual! Sedate!
> Bold as a Brigand!   (P–153)

Like the frost's, his work is irreversible, and so the gestures of grief the mourner offers

> Were useless as next morning's sun–
> Where midnight frosts–had lain!   (P–205)

The lifeless body, dispossessed even of gender in its new state, yet becomes of greatest worth when lost. Its value grows

> Vast–in it's fading ratio
> To our penurious eyes!   (P–88)

Emily Dickinson's obsessive recognition of the absolute disjunction which death causes demanded the creation of a new word for the condition of the dead, who exist

> . . . while we stare,
> In Leagueless Opportunity,
> O'ertakeless, as the Air.   (P–282)

Her scrutiny of nature, like her scrutiny of the moment of death, also evoked brilliant expressions. That close investigation of the things of this world, she implies in the much-quoted quatrain defining the utility of faith, is what sustains one who does not accept the specious comfort of strong belief:

> "Faith" is a fine invention
> When Gentlemen can see–
> But *Microscopes* are prudent
> In an Emergency.   (P–185)

The recurrent mysteriousness of the changing seasons is one quality that engages the imagination, evading rational comprehension:

> If Summer were *an Axiom*–
> What sorcery had *Snow*?   (P–191)

And in other lines she asserts her habitual regard for the familiar seasonal signs:

> Without the Snow's Tableau
> Winter, were lie–to me.   (P–285)

Images of summer she selected and rendered in expressive metaphors. She speaks of "An axe shrill singing in the woods" (P–140) and of "Butterflies . . . On their passage Cashmere" (P–86). Early summer is the time when nature takes up its characteristic music, when

> Lethargic pools resume the whirr
> Of last year's sundered tune!   (P–64)

The summer snake's darting motion through the grass, the precise movement of which is the only visible sign of him, strikes immediate fear in the observer:

> Did but a snake bisect the brake
> My life had forfeit been. (P–11)

Emily Dickinson's visionary apprehension of the ideal afterlife is objectified in the personification of nature. The dancing on that "remoter green" is

> As if the stars some summer night
> Should swing their cups of Chrysolite–
> And revel till the day. (P–24)

The "Western Mystery" of the sunset with its continually changing cloud patterns and exotic colors on the horizon she describes metaphorically as a wharf standing by nature's celestial ships from the Orient:

> Night after Night
> Her purple traffic
> Strews the landing with Opal Bales. (P–266)

Her rendering of the emotion of great exultation is by way of the apt metaphor of church bells proclaiming military victory:

> . . . Bells keep saying 'Victory'
> From steeples in my soul! (P–103)

The opposite, the condition of incredible torment confined within a single body, is neatly conveyed in the combined metaphors of the small boring tool (gimlet) and the predatory panther, as well as in the implicit suggestion that at such times one's body seems to be a single receptive nerve:

> . . . Gimblets–among the nerve–
> Mangle daintier–terribler–
> Like a Panther in the Glove. (P–244)

For the finely managed, intrinsic control of despair she employs a military figure. Psychic confrontation with the killing forces of desperation is a kind of heroism; those people engaged in that inner struggle, she says, are

> . . . *gallanter*, I know
> Who charge within the bosom
> The Cavalry of Wo.   (P–126)

The precarious balance between the contrary ideals of spiritual chasteness and absolute selflessness is negotiated in the simple image of the snowflake. Addressing her lover, the speaker pleads that he

> . . . hallow just the snow
> Intact, in Everlasting flake–
> Oh, Caviler, for you!   (P–275)

Remembrance of an earlier love returns vividly in the reading of the preserved love letters with their

> . . . faded syllables
> That quickened us like Wine!   (P–169)

Death of the lover may seem to eradicate those past experiences, however,

> . . . as if no plight
> Had printed yesterday,
> In tender–solemn Alphabet.   (P–263)

Finally, Emily Dickinson in her early career was able to declare sharply and with great economy the attitude of disdain for public recognition. Her choice of the simile of the lowly frog conveys that tone with simple directness:

> How dreary–to be–Somebody!
> How public–like a Frog–
> To tell your name–the livelong June–
> To an admiring Bog!   (P–288)

These varied examples of her fresh and arresting technique, however, are little more than dissociated fragments of her genius. The poems in which this artistry is sustained are the superior achievements and, indeed, are the ultimate products of those early attempts at refining an authentic voice. In drawing attention below to the early works of thorough artistry, many of which are discussed in preceding sections, I have necessarily limited my remarks to those elements which constitute the principal effectiveness in the individual poems.[2]

Of the works embodying the subject of death, at least ten are superior renditions: the earliest is "There's something quieter than sleep" (P-45). Its impact issues from the frugal but suggestive imagery of the dead body and the conventions of mourning, and from the dramatic situation constructed about the three "characters" — the corpse, the mourners, and the speaker. Each has a distinct role, and the contrasts in their three responses to death produce a complex tension. The corpse is inert, yet the focal point of interest; the mourners busily make the conventional gestures of grief over "the early dead," while the speaker frankly confesses she understands neither the fact of death nor the mourners' reaction to it. The central perception, wonderfully understated, is that even in its absolute simplicity death defies comprehension:

> It has a simple gravity
> I do not understand!

Since the speaker cannot cope rationally with the fact of death, as the other mourners seem able to do, she evades it with the laconic but telling observation that the birds have migrated. As readers, we come with almost embarrassing suddenness upon an intimate nervousness that discloses the mind's effort to cohere in the face of final mysteries.

"I never lost as much but twice" (P-49) stands among those poems which convey an emotional intensity seemingly out of all proportion to the magnitude of the statement. Its success is in the stark rendering of the gamut of emotional responses to bereavement. The feelings compounded are those of grief, of bitterness, of indecision, and resignation. This range is effectively expressed through the metaphors of crime and commerce, each of which gives way abruptly to the final humility implied in the paternal address.

> Burglar! Banker–Father!
> I am poor once more!

In briefest possible compass (compare "Lycidas," "In Memoriam," for example) the poet has presented dramatically the transformation of the speaker's attitude from outrage and defiance to humble acquiescence.

"Some things that fly there be" (P–89), discussed earlier as a central document of Emily Dickinson's theme, concentrates its force in the symbols, in the direct fusion of object and idea, which together pose the riddle of time and eternity. In "Went up a year this evening!" (P–93), also discussed earlier, the miracle of the dead rising up is dramatically rendered. The force of the poem resides in the artful combination of fear and wonderment as responses to the spectacle of death. The poet successfully avoids conventional solemnity, creating the more authentic emotion the more effectively by inducing it obliquely. In "I'm 'wife'–I've finished that" (P–199), she expresses a similar awe to dramatize the experience of achieving maturity through crucial experience. The recognition of new status is effectively conveyed in the terms of coronation and the sacrament of marriage. The integrity of the perception locates the pain-pleasure paradox that crucial and irrevocable alteration of one's condition, even to a more desirable state, involves contrary feelings; that whatever now is gained is necessarily at the price of commensurate loss.

Another early poem of considerable skill is "If your Nerve, deny you" (P–292). It presents with cutting wit the dilemma of the mortal state, where spirit and flesh are attracted to polar ends. To the nerves the ideal state is absolute inertia, and this is to be accomplished only in the grave:

> That's a steady posture–
> Never any bend.

The ideal state of the soul, however, is freedom to fly up in resurrection. This basic material of life's tragedy is skillfully distanced from a sentimental handling by a careful measure of humor:

> If your Nerve, deny you–
> Go above your Nerve–
> He can lean against the Grave,
> If he fear to swerve–
>
> That's a steady posture–
> Never any bend
> Held of those Brass arms–
> Best Giant made–
>
> If your Soul seesaw–
> Lift the Flesh door–
> The Poltroon wants Oxygen–
> Nothing more.

The rhyme pattern frames the argument, providing exact harmony in the opening and closing stanzas where the ideal teleology of the flesh and spirit is stated. In the central stanza, however, which recognizes that death is the only resolution and which describes the frightful prison of the grave, the suspended rhyme is properly disconcerting. It provides an audible quality for the less than ideal manner by which the body can avoid anguish.

"One dignity delays for all" (P–98) has been treated in detail earlier. It is enough here to reiterate that its artistry is manifested principally in the sustained identity between the imagery of a coronation and a funeral, and in the superb irony which underlies the statement the poem makes. Life's only dignity may well reside, the poem implies, in the ritual observance of life's end. The apparent consolation for death, consequently, is finally overwhelmed by the surging condemnation of life. "I like a look of Agony" (P–241) strikes us by the way it works out justification for the shocking callousness of the opening line. The poem's residual attitude is not cynicism but rather simple candor in the recognition that death is the ultimate novelty and cannot be feigned. The cruel opening is immediately retrieved by the second line, and then justified in the third and fourth lines:

> I like a look of Agony,
> Because I know it's true—
> Men do not sham Convulsion,
> Nor simulate, a Throe.

In the poem as a whole, death finds its precise definition by the homely details of its physical appearance. Less well known is "That after Horror–that 'twas *us*" (P–286). It recreates the speaker's reaction to a near-confrontation with death. The metaphor of drowning and the novel imagery of the dispassionate mask of death provide effective body, ironically, to "The very profile of the Thought" which, the speaker says, "Puts Recollection numb."

> That after Horror–that 'twas *us*—
> That passed the mouldering Pier—
> Just as the Granite Crumb let go—
> Our Savior, by a Hair—
> A second more, had dropped too deep
> For Fisherman to plumb—
> The very profile of the Thought
> Puts Recollection numb—

> The possibility–to pass
> Without a Moment's Bell–
> Into Conjecture's presence–
> Is like a Face of Steel–
> That suddenly looks into our's
> With a metallic grin–
> The Cordiality of Death–
> Who drills his Welcome in.

The helpless near-victims and the grisly figure of death perform against the background of the ideal implied by the common meter pattern; the horror is intensified by the contrast. We recognize the same effect in the more horrendous nursery rhymes where gruesome tales are the more macabre for rocking along in jump-rope rhythm.

Perhaps her most artful metaphorical excursion in the early period is to be found in the poem "A Clock stopped" (P–287). The figure of man as a clock puppet conveys the satirical recognition that man lives his "Dial life" according to the gestures of a clock face. The tragic knowledge is that the force is inhuman, with power neither to create nor restore the life it tyrannizes. The poem once again proclaims the absolute change that death effects: when man dies into another life, into a scheme of time-lessness, no skill of this earth can call him back from "Degreeless Noon," through the "Decades of Arrogance" to this "Dial life" again:

> A Clock stopped–
> Not the Mantel's–
> Geneva's farthest skill
> Cant put the puppet bowing–
> That just now dangled still–
>
> An awe came on the Trinket!
> The Figures hunched, with pain–
> Then quivered out of Decimals–
> Into Degreeless Noon–

> It will not stir for Doctor's–
> This Pendulum of snow–
> The Shopman importunes it–
> While cool–concernless No–
>
> Nods from the Gilded pointers–
> Nods from the Seconds slim–
> Decades of Arrogance between
> The Dial life–
> And Him.

This poem slays with stunning directness the cozy dream of re-capturing what is lost to time by turning back the clock. Out of that cliché Emily Dickinson compounded a telling commentary on man's routine of life, the drama of his death, and the nature of the immensity of that change.

Her obsessive concern with the moment when the activity of this life dies into soundless inactivity engendered the well-known early poem "Safe in their Alabaster Chambers." (For analysis I use the superior version [P–216; *Poems*, I, 154] which the poet enclosed in her first letter to Higginson.) The work is yet another treatment of the subject of death, of the aspiration of the dead for immortality, and of the riddle of those that resting, rise. It possesses the characteristic emphasis on motion and stasis which informs so much of her poetry. Here the contrast is clearly drawn, providing the structure for the work. Indeed, the mature artistry of the poet is evident in the severe imagery of the stillness of the tomb in contrast to the incessant motion in the universe outside. The effective force of the poem arises from this contrast and from the brilliant closing simile in which the motion in the second stanza is arrested in the snow image, which in turn directs the reader back again to the cold repose of the tomb with which the poem opens. Promise and denial, forever inseparable, are symbolized by the bright satin beneath the impassable stone:

Safe in their Alabaster Chambers–
Untouched by Morning–
And untouched by Noon–
Sleep the meek members of the Resurrection,
Rafter of Satin–and Roof of Stone–

Grand go the Years,
In the Crescent above them–
Worlds scoop their Arcs–
And Firmaments–row–
Diadems–drop–
And Doges–surrender–
Soundless as Dots,
On a Disc of Snow.

The intrinsic control of movement within the poem yet allows
an element of abiding tension created by the residual skepticism
and uneasiness. For though the cycle of life is completed within
the poem there is no assurance that the dead will indeed rise up
to their supposed reward. They are the opposite of "grand" (as
the world goes); they are "untouched" as yet by immortality.
The discomfiture is sounded in the rhyme scheme, for in the
opening stanza which describes the tomb where resurrection is
as yet unachieved, the rhyme is only approximate. In contrast,
the resolving function of the image of snow at the end is reinforced by the exact rhyme. Having encountered the apparent
resolution, however, the reader is directed back by both sound
and image correspondence to the opening stanza. He is turned
back, that is, to the tension at the beginning. In the brief compass of thirteen lines the poet distills life and death, gathers the
one into the other, leaving unresolved the promise of immortality. Elsewhere she describes this tension as

. . . Gravity–and Expectation–and Fear–
A tremor just, that All's not sure.   (P-408)

Other early poems of superior achievement cluster about the
idea that the worth of an experience is ultimately best measured

by those who are denied gratification in it. The central paradox is that in equal ratio to the suffering caused by denial one receives an increased comprehension. "Our lives are Swiss" (P–80) is a succinct rendering of this conception and perhaps one of the best-known examples from her early work. A less well-known early poem of mature skill is also addressed to this subject. Though the work, "If *He dissolve*–then–there is *nothing–more*" (P–236), referred to in a previous section, is weakened by the conventional imagery at its close, the opening is nowhere in her canon surpassed for its intense rendering of the experience of separation. The loss of the lover is "*Eclipse*–at *Midnight*," "*Sunset*–at *Easter*," and "*Blindness*–on the *Dawn*." The metaphors are wide-ranging and consequently imply the magnitude of the grief. "I've known a Heaven, like a Tent" (P–243) and "Unto like Story–Trouble has enticed me" (P–295) are also early achievements of a high order. Each has been discussed earlier in this study. The effective force in the first poem is created in large part through the sustained and novel metaphors for lost faith — the fleeing tent and the staring gesture. The art of the second poem is evidenced principally in the tight control the speaker has over her centrifugal emotions. The discipline of emotion dramatized within the poem is reflected in the compactness of the expression. Like the speaker's emotions, the poet's close articulation is "Drilled bright." The best known of the poems about compensation is undoubtedly "Success is counted sweetest" (P–67). It is also one of her finest works from the early years. The value of fulfillment, the poem declares, is understood fully only by those who are denied it. The argument is superbly rendered in the metaphor with which the poem closes: it is only the dead ear, paradoxically, that hears most clearly the music of triumph.

The group of early poems of mature artistry which focus on nature as spectacle and as symbol of the aspirer's goal includes poems already discussed: "There's a certain Slant of light" (P–

258), "On this long storm the Rainbow rose" (P–194), and "An awful Tempest mashed the air" (P–198). The skill in these poems lies principally in the choice of imagery and in the way familiar experience is recreated in novel perspective. "These are the days when Birds come back" (P–130) succeeds in its creation of the devotional tone; we are engaged in the dramatic transformation of the speaker's attitude from her initial awareness of the deception of nature (in its Indian summer days) to her final capitulation when the emotional pressures of desire triumph over reason, and she humbly seeks to participate in the "Sacrament of summer days." In this general subject area, too, is the much-anthologized "I taste a liquor never brewed" (P–214). The whole sense of the poem is that in nature one may find the stimulants for intemperate joy. The engaging qualities of this poem are not, of course, in the hackneyed notion that nature is the aliment of happiness. Rather, those qualities issue from Emily Dickinson's wit in appropriating nature imagery to the underlying metaphor of inebriation. The ultimate triumph of her virtuoso performance in this poem is that she sings the scandalous behavior of the speaker (perhaps a bumblebee, but very unlike Emerson's) in the stately rhythms of the common meter of hymnody.

The remaining early works in which we discover Emily Dickinson's profoundest skill are brilliant studies in the psychology of emotional discipline. "A *Wounded* Deer–leaps highest" (P–165), "I can wade Grief" (P–252), "'Hope' is the thing with feathers" (P–254), and "One Year ago–jots what?" (P–296) have been discussed earlier in this study. In general, their effectiveness derives from exact imagery, from highly concentrated expression, and from their communication of emotional complexity. On the experience of psychic breakdown, perhaps no poetic expression surpasses the aptness of metaphor or the psychological authenticity of the progression of mental collapse as the rightly famous "I felt a Funeral, in my Brain" (P–280). In addition, certain of her finest early works deal conversely with the stoical ideal of controlled emotions and of the power to be possessed from pain. Though "I have never seen 'Volcanoes'" (P–175) is one of these superior poems, it has had little critical regard. Its effectiveness springs from the sustained and perfectly appropriate adoption of the volcano metaphor to embody the idea of intense emotions under deliberate control:

> I have never seen 'Volcanoes'–
> But, when Travellers tell
> How those old–phlegmatic mountains
> Usually so still–
>
> Bear within–appalling Ordnance,
> Fire, and smoke, and gun,
> Taking Villages for breakfast,
> And appalling Men–
>
> If the stillness is Volcanic
> In the human face
> When upon a pain Titanic
> Features keep their place–
>
> If at length, the smouldering anguish
> Will not overcome–
> And the palpitating Vineyard
> In the dust, be thrown?
>
> If some loving Antiquary,
> On Resumption Morn,
> Will not cry with joy "Pompeii"!
> To the Hills return!

The extended comparison in the geological-emotional analogue moves deftly toward the climactic, assured attitude epitomized in the final heretical viewpoint. The speaker declares triumphantly that if God (the "loving Antiquary") won't allow even on Judgment Day the wished-for purgation of pent-up anguish, then through eternity she is capable of concealing the pain. While the poem's apparent goal has been to render a final and divinely sanctioned emotional eruption, its profounder purpose has been to characterize the triumph of the stoical self.

A similar sort of heresy animates "I got so I could hear his name" (P–293), another early work of consummate artistry. By the fourth stanza, having by painfully slow degrees and great effort become sufficiently detached from the anguishing experience of separation from a loved one, the speaker is able to contemplate an attempt for comfort in prayer, even though it is an unfamiliar gesture. We see how the soul's agony is made vivid by the imagery of physical pain:

> I got so I could hear his name–
> Without–Tremendous gain–
> That Stop-sensation–on my Soul–
> And Thunder–in the Room–
>
> I got so I could walk across
> That Angle in the floor,
> Where he turned so, and I turned–how–
> And all our Sinew tore–
>
> I got so I could stir the Box–
> In which his letters grew
> Without that forcing, in my breath–
> As Staples–driven through–
>
> Could dimly recollect a Grace–
> I think, they call it "God"–
> Renowned to ease Extremity–
> When Formula, had failed–
>
> And shape my Hands–
> Petition's way,
> Tho' ignorant of a word
> That Ordination–utters.

Having so effectively brought emotional disturbance under control, the speaker in the final stanza rejects the thought of plead-

ing for divine aid, for, she believes, though she prays to the
ultimate power, if that power has not also known despair it can
offer comfort only in some disinterested and ineffectual way.
The ultimate power may consider her misery trivial, but to her
that "minute affair" of anguish is so enormous it excludes any
sort of interruption, including (she says finally) even the offering
up of prayer:

> My Business, with the Cloud,
> If any Power behind it, be,
> Not subject to Despair—
> It care, in some remoter way,
> For so minute affair
> As Misery—
> Itself, too great, for interrupting—more.

Reading the first line of this last excerpt as if it ended with a
period clarifies the meaning. The fusion of agonizing experiences,
mental and physical, the sharp metaphorical depiction of pain,
and the articulation of how the person is ravished by the experience of loss — how first the physical senses respond, then the
emotions, then the mind, as each is in turn called back to activity from paralysis — are highly effective. The vision is a tragic
one: even if God is attentive to individual anguish, He is effec-
tually indifferent.

In this poem, as in the other works referred to in this chapter,
Emily Dickinson's genius clearly had guided her expression beyond the level of conventional sentiment and emotional cliché
to the level of mature poetry. In the years from 1850 to 1862 she
succeeded in refining genuine and effective expressions of feeling from a clutter of commonplace ideas and syntaxes. Perhaps
the principal reason for her early success is that she addressed
herself again and again to a single theme. The repeated application not only deepened her psychological insight, but allowed
her opportunities to pursue a variety of attitudes and to refine
her expression. That refinement is evidenced in a wide range

of elements, but most obviously perhaps in her imagery and in her prosodic variations on the hymn patterns that provided her metrical base. The development of irony she was able to maintain effectively through the speaker's vigorously secular attitude and through meaningful manipulations of sound correspondences.

But ultimately the totality of her art in the early years is greater than the sum of the individual elements that go into its makeup. Her expressive skills combined to effect a concision, a specific gravity, as it were, not often encountered in English poetry. Her elliptic expression is all the more remarkable for embodying the complexity which it does. That complexity and the intensity of the feeling with which she informs her best works from this period are, in turn, the more remarkable for being under firm control. Long before she wrote to Higginson to inquire if her poetry "breathed," Emily Dickinson had reached on several occasions that high level of lyric expression at which extraordinary emotional impulses are matched and dominated by even more extraordinary discipline. Beyond this accomplishment, she had by 1862 developed her unique ability to dissociate feelings from the limitations of specific causal experiences. Her poems exist independent of the confining facts of exterior experience, and become thereby increasingly universal. She distilled the essential psychic responses to experience — those feelings that are communicable most fully intact. That she displayed this consummate artistry in a substantial body of early work, and that in an even greater number of poems she successfully experimented in usages outside the poetic conventions of her time, provides irrefutable testimony to the judgment that she composed with purpose and conviction.[3] Her assurance of her poetic capability is evidenced most profoundly by these early performances, which fulfill the artistic promise in her response to Higginson's "Letter to a Young Contributor" and in the poems she enclosed.

SELECTED BIBLIOGRAPHY

Primary Works

Dickinson, Emily. *A Concordance to the Poems of Emily Dickinson*, ed. S. P. Rosenbaum. Ithaca: Cornell University Press, 1964.

—— *Bolts of Melody: New Poems of Emily Dickinson*, ed. Mabel L. Todd and Millicent T. Bingham. New York: Harper, 1945.

—— *Emily Dickinson's Letters to Dr. and Mrs. Josiah Gilbert Holland*, ed. Theodora Ward. Cambridge, Mass.: Harvard University Press, 1951.

—— *Final Harvest: Emily Dickinson's Poems*, ed. Thomas H. Johnson. Boston and Toronto: Little, Brown, 1961.

—— *Further Poems of Emily Dickinson Withheld from Publication by Her Sister Lavinia*, ed. Martha D. Bianchi and Alfred L. Hampson. Boston: Little, Brown, 1929.

—— *Letters of Emily Dickinson*, ed. Mabel L. Todd. 2 vols. Boston: Roberts Brothers, 1894.

—— *Letters of Emily Dickinson*, ed. Mabel L. Todd. N.p.: World Publishing Co., 1951.

—— *The Letters of Emily Dickinson*, ed. Thomas H. Johnson. 3 vols. Cambridge, Mass.: Harvard University Press, 1958.

—— *Poems by Emily Dickinson*, ed. Mabel L. Todd. Third Series. Boston: Roberts Brothers, 1896.

—— *Poems by Emily Dickinson Edited by Two of Her Friends*, ed. Mabel L. Todd and T. W. Higginson. Boston: Roberts Brothers, 1890.

—— *Poems by Emily Dickinson Edited by Two of Her Friends*, ed. T. W. Higginson and Mabel L. Todd. Second Series. Boston: Roberts Brothers, 1891.

—— *Poems of Emily Dickinson*, ed. Louis Untermeyer. New York: Heritage Press, 1952.

—— *The Poems of Emily Dickinson: Including variant readings critically compared with all known manuscripts*, ed. Thomas H. Johnson. 3 vols. Cambridge, Mass.: Harvard University Press, 1958.

—— *Selected Poems of Emily Dickinson*, ed. Conrad Aiken. London: Jonathan Cape, 1924.

—— *The Single Hound: Poems of a Lifetime*, ed. Martha D. Bianchi. Boston: Little, Brown, 1914.

—— *Unpublished Poems of Emily Dickinson*, ed. Martha D. Bianchi and Alfred L. Hampson. Boston: Little, Brown, 1935.

Emily Dickinson December 10, 1830–May 15, 1886. A Bibliography.
The Jones Library, Inc., Amherst, Mass., 1930.

Biographical Works

Bianchi, Martha D. *Emily Dickinson Face to Face: Unpublished Letters
with Notes and Reminiscences.* Boston: Houghton Mifflin, 1932.
———*The Life and Letters of Emily Dickinson by Her Niece.* Boston:
Houghton Mifflin, 1924.
Bingham, Millicent T. *Ancestors' Brocades: The Literary Debut of
Emily Dickinson.* New York: Harper, 1945.
———*Emily Dickinson: A Revelation.* New York: Harper, 1954.
———*Emily Dickinson's Home: Letters of Edward Dickinson and His
Family with Documentation and Comment.* New York: Harper,
1955.
Chase, Richard. *Emily Dickinson.* New York: Wm. Sloane, 1951.
Jenkins, MacGregor. *Emily Dickinson: Friend and Neighbor.* Boston:
Little, Brown, 1930.
Johnson, Thomas H. *Emily Dickinson: An Interpretive Biography.*
Cambridge, Mass.: Harvard University Press, 1955.
———"The Great Love in the Life of Emily Dickinson," *American Heri-
tage,* 6:52–55 (April 1955).
Leyda, Jay. *The Years and Hours of Emily Dickinson.* 2 vols. New
Haven: Yale University Press, 1960.
Ward, Theodora. *The Capsule of the Mind: Chapters in the Life of
Emily Dickinson.* Cambridge, Mass.: Harvard University Press,
1961.
Whicher, G. F. *This Was A Poet: A Critical Biography of Emily Dickin-
son.* New York: Scribner's, 1938.

Critical and General Works

Abrams, M. H. *The Mirror and the Lamp: Romantic Theory and the
Critical Tradition.* New York: Oxford University Press, 1953.
Adams, Richard P. "Pure Poetry: Emily Dickinson," *Tulane Studies in
English.* 7:133–152 (1957).
Allen, Gay Wilson. *American Prosody.* N. p.: American Book Company,
1935.
Anderson, Charles R. "The Conscious Self in Emily Dickinson's Poetry,"
American Literature, 31:290–308 (November 1959).
———*Emily Dickinson's Poetry: Stairway of Surprise.* New York: Holt,
Rinehart and Winston, 1960.
———"From a Window in Amherst: Emily Dickinson Looks at the
American Scene," *New England Quarterly,* 31:147–171 (June
1958).

———— "The Trap of Time in Emily Dickinson's Poetry," *Journal of English Literary History*, 26:402–424 (September 1959).

Anthony, Mother Mary. "Emily Dickinson's Scriptural Echoes," *Massachusetts Review*, 2:557–561 (Spring 1961).

Baldi, Sergio. "The Poetry of Emily Dickinson (1956)," *Sewanee Review*, 68:438–449 (July–September 1960).

Banzer, Judith. "'Compound Manner': Emily Dickinson and the Metaphysical Poets," *American Literature*, 32:417–433 (January 1961).

Barbot, Mary E. "Emily Dickinson Parallels," *New England Quarterly*, 14:689–696 (December 1941).

Bingham, Millicent T. "Emily Dickinson's Handwriting — A Master Key," *New England Quarterly*, 22:229–234 (June 1949).

Birdsall, Virginia O. "Emily Dickinson's Intruder in the Soul," *American Literature*, 37:54–64 (March 1965).

Blackmur, R. P. "Emily Dickinson: Notes on Prejudice and Fact" in *The Expense of Greatness*. New York: Arrow, 1940.

———— "Emily Dickinson's Notation," *Kenyon Review*, 18: 224–237 (1956).

———— *Language As Gesture*. New York: Harcourt, Brace, 1952.

———— "Religious Poetry in America," *University — A Princeton Magazine*, 9:14–19 (Summer 1961).

Blake, Caesar R. and C. F. Wells, eds. *The Recognition of Emily Dickinson: Selected Criticism Since 1890*. Ann Arbor: University of Michigan Press, 1964.

Bogan, Louise. "A Mystical Poet," in *Emily Dickinson: Three Views*. Amherst, Mass.: Amherst College Press, 1960.

Bostetter, Edward E. *The Romantic Ventriloquists: Wordsworth, Coleridge, Keats, Shelley, Byron*. Seattle: University of Washington Press, 1963.

Bowra, C. M. *The Romantic Imagination*. Cambridge, Mass.: Harvard University Press, 1949.

Brooks, Van Wyck. *New England: Indian Summer 1865–1915*. New York: Dutton, 1940.

Brown, Norman O. *Life Against Death*. Middletown, Conn.: Wesleyan University Press, 1959.

Cambon, Glauco. "Violence and Abstraction in Emily Dickinson (1958)," *Sewanee Review*, 68:450–464 (July–September 1960).

Capps, Jack L. "Emily Dickinson's Reading 1836–1886: A Study of the Sources of Her Poetry," unpub. diss., University of Pennsylvania, 1963.

Carpenter, Frederic I. "Emily Dickinson and the Rhymes of Dream," *University of Kansas City Review*, 20:113–120 (1953).

Childs, Herbert E. "Emily Dickinson and Sir Thomas Browne," *American Literature*, 22:455–465 (1951).

Childs, Herbert E. "Emily Dickinson, Spinster," *Western Humanities Review*, 3:303–309 (1949).

Connors, Donald F. "The Significance of Emily Dickinson," *College English*, 3:624–633 (1942).

Davidson, Edward H. *Poe: A Critical Study*. Cambridge, Mass.: Belknap Press of Harvard University Press, 1957.

Davidson, Frank. "A Note on Emily Dickinson's Use of Shakespeare," *New England Quarterly*, 18:407–408 (September 1945).

Davidson, James. "Emily Dickinson and Isaac Watts," *Boston Public Library Quarterly*, 6:141–149 (July 1954).

Deutsch, Babette. "Miracle and Mystery," *Poetry*, 66:274–280 (August 1945).

Edwards, Jonathan. *Images or Shadows of Divine Things*, ed. Perry Miller. New Haven: Yale University Press, 1948.

Eliot, T. S. "The Poetry of W. B. Yates," in *The Permanence of Yeats: Selected Criticism*, ed. James Hall and Martin Steinmann. New York: Macmillan, 1950.

Emerson, Ralph W. *Poems*. Boston: James Munroe, 1847.

"Emily Dickinson, The Domestication of Terror," *Times Literary Supplement* (London), September 9, 1955, p. 532.

England, Martha W. "Emily Dickinson and Isaac Watts: Puritan Hymnodists," *Bulletin of the New York Public Library*, 69:83–116 (February 1965).

Fain, John T. "'New Poems' of Emily Dickinson," *Modern Language Notes*, 68:112–113 (January 1953).

Foote, Henry Wilder. *Three Centuries of American Hymnody*. Cambridge, Mass.: Harvard University Press, 1940.

Friedman, Norman. *e. e. cummings: the art of his poetry*. Baltimore: Johns Hopkins University Press, 1960.

Gelpi, Albert J. *Emily Dickinson — The Mind of the Poet*. Cambridge, Mass.: Harvard University Press, 1965.

Gleckner, Robert F. *The Piper and the Bard: A Study of William Blake*. Detroit: Wayne State University Press, 1959.

Glenn, Eunice. "Emily Dickinson's Poetry: A Revaluation," *Sewanee Review*, 51:574–588 (Autumn 1943).

Goethe, Johann. *Faust*, Part One, trans. Philip Wayne. Baltimore: Penguin Books, 1961.

Gombrich, E. H. *Art and Illusion: A Study in the Psychology of Pictorial Representation*. New York: Pantheon, 1961.

——— *Meditations on a Hobby Horse and Other Essays on the Theory of Art*. Greenwich, Conn.: Phaidon, 1964.

Goodrich, Samuel G. *Peter Parley's Farewell*. Philadelphia, 1841.

Graves, L. B. "The Likeness of Emily Dickinson," *Harvard Library Bulletin*, 1:248–251 (Spring 1947).

Gregory, Horace. "The Real Emily Dickinson," *Commonweal*, 68:449–450 (August 1958).

Grierson, H. J. C. *Lyrical Poetry of the Nineteenth Century*. New York: Harcourt, Brace, 1929.

Griffith, Clark. "Emily Dickinson's Love Poetry," *University of Kansas City Review*, 27:93–100 (1960).

—— *The Long Shadow: Emily Dickinson's Tragic Poetry*. Princeton: Princeton University Press, 1964.

Hicks, Granville. *The Great Tradition: An Interpretation of American Literature Since the Civil War*. New York: Macmillan, 1933.

Higgins, David J. M. "Portrait of Emily Dickinson: The Poet and Her Prose," *Dissertation Abstracts*, 22:246–247 (1961).

Higginson, Mary Thacher. *Thomas Wentworth Higginson*. Boston: Houghton Mifflin, 1914.

Higginson, T. W. "Emily Dickinson's Letters," *Atlantic Monthly*, 68:444–456 (October 1891).

—— "Letter to a Young Contributor," *Atlantic Monthly*, 9:401–411 (April 1862).

Hindus, Milton. "Emily's Prose: A Note," *Kenyon Review*, 2:88–91 (1940).

Howard, Mabel, William Howard, and Emily Harvey. "Dickinson's 'My Wheel is in the Dark,'" *Explicator*, 17, Item 12 (October 1958–June 1959).

Howard, William. "Dickinson's 'I Can Wade Grief,'" *Explicator*, 14, Item 17 (December 1955).

—— "Dickinson's 'Safe in Their Alabaster Chambers,'" *Explicator*, 17, Item 62 (October 1958–June 1959).

—— "Emily Dickinson's Poetic Vocabulary," *PMLA*, 72:225–248 (March 1957).

Ing, Catherine. *Elizabethan Lyrics: A Study in the Development of English Metres and their Relation to Poetic Effect*. London: Chatto and Windus, 1951.

Jennings, Elizabeth. "Emily Dickinson and the Poetry of the Inner Life," *A Review of English Literature*, 3:78–87 (April 1962).

Johnson, Thomas H. "Emily Dickinson: Creating the Poems," *Harvard Library Bulletin*, 7:257–270 (Autumn 1953).

—— "Establishing a Text: The Emily Dickinson Papers," *Studies in Bibliography*, 5:21–32 (1952–1953).

Jones, Rowena Revis. "Emily Dickinson's 'Flood Subject': Immortality," *Dissertation Abstracts*, 21:1554–55 (1960).

Keats, John. *The Letters of John Keats 1814–1821*, ed. H. E. Rollins. 2 vols. Cambridge, Mass.: Harvard University Press, 1958.

Kelcher, Julia. "The Enigma of Emily Dickinson," *New Mexico Quarterly*, 2:326–332 (November 1932).

Langer, Susanne K. *Philosophy in A New Key: A Study in the Symbolism of Reason, Rite, and Art.* 3rd ed. Cambridge, Mass.: Harvard University Press, 1957.

Lenhart, Charmenz S. *Musical Influence on American Poetry.* Athens, Ga.: University of Georgia Press, 1956.

Leyda, Jay. "Late Thaw of a Frozen Image," *New Republic,* February 21, 1955, pp. 22–24.

——— "Miss Emily's Maggie," in *New World Writing,* Third Mentor Selection. New York, 1953.

Lowell, Amy. *Poetry and Poets.* Boston: Houghton Mifflin, 1930.

MacLean, Kenneth. "The Mail from Tunis," *University of Toronto Quarterly,* 20:27–32 (October 1950).

MacLeish, Archibald. *Poetry and Experience.* Boston: Houghton Mifflin, 1961.

——— "The Private World" in *Emily Dickinson: Three Views.* Amherst, Mass.: Amherst College Press, 1960.

Manierre, William R. "E. D.: Visions and Revisions," *Texas Studies in Literature and Language,* 5:5–16 (1963).

Mann, Thomas. *The Magic Mountain,* trans. H. T. Lowe-Porter. New York: Alfred A. Knopf, 1955.

Matchett, William H. "The 'Success' by Emily Dickinson," *Boston Public Library Quarterly,* 8:144–147 (July 1956).

Matthiessen, F. O. "The Problem of the Private Poet," *Kenyon Review,* 7:584–597 (Autumn 1945).

Maurois, André. "Emily Dickinson, Poétesse et recluse," *Revue de Paris,* 60:1–13 (November 1954).

McNaughton, R. F. "Emily Dickinson on Death," *Prairie Schooner,* 23: 203–215 (Summer 1949).

——— *The Imagery of Emily Dickinson.* Lincoln, Nebraska: University of Nebraska Press, 1949.

Merideth, Robert. "Emily Dickinson and the Acquisitive Society," *New England Quarterly,* 37:435–452 (December 1964).

Meyer, Leonard B. *Emotion and Meaning in Music.* Chicago: University of Chicago Press, 1956.

Miller, Betty. "Elizabeth and Emily Elizabeth," *Twentieth Century,* 49: 574–583 (June 1956).

Miller, James E., Jr. "Emily Dickinson: The Thunder's Tongue," *Minnesota Review,* 2:289–304 (Spring 1962).

Miller, Perry. "Jonathan Edwards to Emerson," *New England Quarterly,* 13:589–617 (December 1940).

——— et al., eds. *Major Writers of America.* 2 vols. New York: Harcourt, Brace, 1962.

——— *The New England Mind from Colony to Province.* Cambridge, Mass.: Harvard University Press, 1953.

Miner, E. R. "Dickinson's 'A Clock Stopped — Not the Mantel's,'" *Explicator*, 13, Item 18 (December 1954).

Monteiro, George. "Traditional Ideas in Dickinson's 'I Felt a Funeral in My Brain,'" *Modern Language Notes*, 75:656–663 (1960).

Moore, Marianne. "Emily Dickinson," *Poetry*, 41:219–226 (January 1933).

Moseley, Edwin. "The Gambit of Emily Dickinson," *University of Kansas City Review*, 16:11–19 (1949).

Ochshorn, Myron. "In Search of Emily Dickinson," *New Mexico Quarterly*, 23:94–106 (Spring 1953).

Parks, Edd Winfield. "The Public and the Private Poet," *South Atlantic Quarterly*, 56:480–485 (Autumn 1957).

Pattee, F. L. "Gentian, Not Rose: The Real Emily Dickinson," *Sewanee Review*, 45:180–197 (April–June 1937).

Patterson, Rebecca. "Emily Dickinson's Palette," *Midwest Quarterly*, 5: 271–291 (Summer 1964).

——— "Emily Dickinson's Palette (II)," *Midwest Quarterly*, 6:97–117 (Autumn 1964).

——— *The Riddle of Emily Dickinson*. Boston: Houghton Mifflin, 1951.

Pearce, R. H. "On the Continuity of American Poetry," *Hudson Review*, 10:518–539 (Winter 1957–1958).

Perkins, David. *Wordsworth and the Poetry of Sincerity*. Cambridge, Mass.: Belknap Press of Harvard University Press, 1964.

Perrine, Lawrence. "Dickinson's 'There's a Certain Slant of Light,'" *Explicator*, 11, Item 50 (May 1953).

Pohl, Frederick J. "The Emily Dickinson Controversy," *Sewanee Review*, 51:467–482 (1933).

Polanyi, Michael. *Personal Knowledge: Towards a Post-Critical Philosophy*. 2nd ed. Chicago: University of Chicago Press, 1960.

Pollitt, Josephine. *Emily Dickinson: The Human Background of Her Poetry*. New York: Harper, 1930.

Poulet, Georges. *Studies in Human Time*, trans. Elliott Coleman. Baltimore: Johns Hopkins University Press, 1956.

Power, Sister Mary James. *In the Name of the Bee: The Significance of Emily Dickinson*. New York: Sheed and Ward, 1943.

Ransom, John Crowe. "Emily Dickinson," *Perspectives USA*, no. 15 (Spring 1956), 5–20.

Robertson, Stuart. *The Development of Modern English*. Revised by Frederic G. Cassidy. Englewood Cliffs, New Jersey: Prentice-Hall, 1961.

Rourke, Constance. *American Humor: A Study of the National Character*. New York: Harcourt, Brace, 1931.

Saintsbury, George. *Historical Manual of English Prosody*. London: Macmillan, 1930.

Santayana, George. *Three Philosophical Poets: Lucretius, Dante, and Goethe.* 3rd ed. Cambridge, Mass.: Harvard University Press, 1922.

Sapir, Edward. "Emily Dickinson, A Primitive," *Poetry,* 26:97–105 (May 1925).

Satterwhite, Joseph N. "Robert Penn Warren and Emily Dickinson," *Modern Language Notes,* 71:347–349 (May 1956).

Schipper, Jakob. *A History of English Versification.* Oxford: Clarendon Press, 1910.

Sessions, I. B. "The Dramatic Monologue," *PMLA,* 62:503–516 (June 1947).

Sewall, Richard B., ed. *Emily Dickinson: A Collection of Critical Essays.* Englewood Cliffs, N. J.: Prentice-Hall, 1963.

——— "On Teaching Emily Dickinson," *The English Leaflet,* 63:3–14 (Spring 1964).

Shackford, Martha H. *Studies of Certain Nineteenth Century Poets.* Natick, Mass.: Suburban Press, 1946.

Sherrer, Grace B. "A Study of Unusual Verb Constructions in the Poems of Emily Dickinson," *American Literature,* 7:37–46 (1935).

Spicer, John L. "The Poems of Emily Dickinson," *Boston Public Library Quarterly,* 8:135–143 (July 1956).

Spiller, Robert E., Willard Thorp, Thomas H. Johnson, and Henry S. Canby, eds. *Literary History of the United States.* 3 vols. 3rd ed. New York: Macmillan, 1963.

Stamm, Edith Perry. "Emily Dickinson: Poetry and Punctuation," *Saturday Review of Literature,* March 30, 1963, pp. 26–27, 74.

Sypher, Wylie. *Rococo to Cubism in Art and Literature.* New York: Random House, 1960.

Taggard, Genevieve. *The Life and Mind of Emily Dickinson.* New York: Knopf, 1930.

Tate, Allen. *Collected Essays.* Denver: Swallow, 1959.

——— "New England Culture and Emily Dickinson," *Symposium,* 3: 206–226 (April 1932).

Thackrey, Donald E. *Emily Dickinson's Approach to Poetry.* Lincoln, Nebraska: University of Nebraska Press, 1954.

Untermeyer, Louis, ed. *Modern American Poetry Mid-Century Edition.* New York: Harcourt, Brace, 1950.

Van Deusen, Marshall. "Dickinson's 'These Are the Days When Birds Come Back,'" *Explicator,* 7, Item 40 (April 1954).

Ward, Theodora. "Emily Dickinson and T. W. Higginson," *Boston Public Library Quarterly,* 5:3–18 (January 1953).

——— "The Finest Secret: Emotional Currents in the Life of Emily Dickinson after 1865," *Harvard Library Bulletin,* 14:82–106 (Winter 1960).

—— "Ourself Behind Ourself: An Interpretation of the Crisis in the Life of Emily Dickinson," *Harvard Library Bulletin*, 10:5–38 (Winter 1956).

Warren, Austin. "Emily Dickinson," *Sewanee Review*, 65:565–586 (1957).

Watts, Isaac. *Isaac Watts Hymns and Spiritual Songs 1707–1748: A Study in Early Eighteenth Century Language Changes*, ed. Selma L. Bishop. London: Faith Press, 1962.

—— *The Psalms, Hymns, and Spiritual Songs, of the Rev. Isaac Watts, D. D. to Which Are Added, Select Hymns from Other Authors; and Directions for Musical Expression*, ed. Samuel Worcester, D. D. Boston, 1827.

—— *The Psalms of David Imitated in the Language of the New Testament, and Adapted to the Christian Use and Worship. By I. Watts, D. D. A New Edition, In Which the Psalms Omitted by Dr. Watts, Are Versified, Local Passages are Altered, And a Number of Psalms are Versified Anew In Proper Metres. By Timothy Dwight, D. D. Late President of Yale College.* . . . *To The Psalms is Added, A Selection of Hymns.* Hartford, Conn.: Gleason, 1830.

—— *Watts's Church Psalmody: A Collection of Psalms and Hymns, Adapted to Public Worship.* Boston, 1854.

Welland, D. S. R. "Half-Rhyme in Wilfred Owen: Its Derivation and Use," *Review of English Studies*, N.S. 1:226–241 (July 1950).

—— *Wilfred Owen: A Critical Study.* London: Chatto and Windus, 1960.

Wellek, René and Austin Warren, *Theory of Literature.* New York: Harcourt, Brace, 1949.

Wells, Anna Mary. *Dear Preceptor: The Life and Times of Thomas Wentworth Higginson.* Boston: Houghton Mifflin, 1963.

—— "Early Criticism of Emily Dickinson," *American Literature*, 1: 243–259 (1929).

Wells, Henry. *Introduction to Emily Dickinson.* Chicago: Hendricks House, 1947.

Wheatcroft, John S. "Emily Dickinson and the Orthodox Tradition," *Dissertation Abstracts*, 21:1186–87 (1960).

Whicher, George F. "A Chronological Grouping of Some of Emily Dickinson's Poems," *The Colophon*, vol. 4 (March 1934), pages unnumbered.

—— "Emily Dickinson's Earliest Friend," *American Literature*, 6:1–17 (March 1934).

—— "In Emily Dickinson's Garden," *Atlantic Monthly*, 177:64–70 (February 1946).

White, William. "Homage to Emily Dickinson: Tributes by Creative

Artists," *Bulletin of Bibliography and Dramatic Index*, 20:112–115 (May–August 1951).

Whiteside, M. B. "Poe and Dickinson," *Personalist*, 15:315–326 (Autumn 1934).

Wilbur, Richard. "Sumptuous Destitution" in *Emily Dickinson: Three Views*. Amherst, Mass.: Amherst College Press, 1960.

Wilder, Thornton. "Emily Dickinson," *Atlantic Monthly*, 190:43–48 (November 1952).

Willy, Margaret. "The Poetry of Emily Dickinson," *Essays and Studies by Members of the English Association*, 10:91–104 (1957).

Wilson, Suzanne M. "Emily Dickinson and Twentieth-Century Poetry of Sensibility," *American Literature*, 36:349–358 (November 1964).

——— "Structural Patterns in the Poetry of Emily Dickinson," *American Literature*, 35:53–59 (March 1963).

——— "Structure and Imagery Patterns in the Poetry of Emily Dickinson," *Dissertation Abstracts*, 20:3286–87 (1960).

Winters, Yvor. "Emily Dickinson and the Limits of Judgment," in *In Defense of Reason*. New York: Swallow Press and W. Morrow, 1947.

"Woman in White, The," *Times Literary Supplement* (London), June 16, 1961, p. 372.

Wright, Nathalia. "Emily Dickinson's Boanerges and Thoreau's Atropos: Locomotives on the Same Line?" *Modern Language Notes*, 72:101–103 (February 1957).

NOTES

CHAPTER I: The Formative Years

1. Citations from Emily Dickinson's poetry are to *The Poems of Emily Dickinson: Including variant readings critically compared with all known manuscripts*, ed. Thomas H. Johnson, 3 vols. (Cambridge, Mass., 1958) — hereafter cited as *Poems*. The poems are consecutively numbered in the Johnson edition and are identified in my text by the notation within parentheses of "P" followed by the number. This epigraph is from "I cannot dance upon my Toes" (P-326).

2. *The Letters of Emily Dickinson*, ed. Thomas H. Johnson, 3 vols. (Cambridge, Mass., 1958), II, 404. Subsequent passages from the letters are from this edition, hereafter cited as *Letters*, and are identified in my text by the notation within parentheses of "L" followed by the Johnson number.

3. Charles R. Anderson, *Emily Dickinson's Poetry: Stairway of Surprise* (New York, 1960) p. xii.

4. Austin Warren, "Emily Dickinson," *Emily Dickinson: A Collection of Critical Essays*, ed. R. B. Sewall (Englewood Cliffs, N.J., 1963), p. 103. The essay is reprinted from *Sewanee Review*, 65:565–586 (1957).

5. Nicholas Joost, "The Pain That Emily Knew," *Poetry*, 80:243 (July 1952).

6. G. F. Whicher, *This Was a Poet: A Critical Biography of Emily Dickinson* (New York, 1938), p. 269.

7. Theodora Ward, *The Capsule of the Mind: Chapters in the Life of Emily Dickinson* (Cambridge, Mass., 1961), p. 39.

8. *Ibid.*, p. vii.

9. *The Complete Poems of Emily Dickinson*, ed. Thomas H. Johnson (Boston, 1960), p. vi. This view appears also in his discussion of the Dickinson-Higginson relationship in *Emily Dickinson: An Interpretive Biography* (Cambridge, Mass., 1955), pp. 103–133.

10. *Letters*, I, xx.

11. Thomas H. Johnson, "Establishing a Text: The Emily Dickinson Papers," *Studies in Bibliography*, 5:22 (1952–1953).

12. *Letters*, I, xix.

13. Northrup Frye, *Major Writers of America*, ed. Perry Miller, *et al.*, 2 vols. (New York, 1962), II, 10. For additional commentary on Emily Dickinson's development as an artist see Richard Chase, *Emily Dickinson* (New York, 1951), p. 101.

14. Thomas Higginson, "Letter to a Young Contributor," *Atlantic Monthly*, 9:410 (April 1862).

15. *Ibid.*, p. 401.

16. *Ibid.*

17. *Ibid.*, p. 404.

18. *Ibid.*, p. 403.

19. *Ibid.*, p. 406.

20. *Ibid.*, p. 410.

21. *Ibid.*, p. 405.

22. Higginson's lectures on behalf of women's rights were well publicized. See Mary Thacher Higginson, *Thomas Wentworth Higginson: The Story of His Life* (Boston, 1914), pp. 137–138.

23. Perhaps other factors also contributed. I tend to agree with the suggestion of Richard B. Sewall that Emily Dickinson's fear of blindness lay near the source of her anxiety at this time. Johnson (*An Interpretive Biography*, pp. 120–121) argues persuasively that in addition to the encouragement in Higginson's article was the poet's need for a "preceptor," for the masculine strength and sympathy she was to lose upon the departure of the Reverend Charles Wadsworth from Philadelphia to accept a call to the Calvary Church in San Francisco. His acceptance of the post had been announced March 15, 1862, and he sailed the following May 1st. That Emily Dickinson required another person to replace this figure of devotion and strength whom she had met in 1854 is justifiable speculation. Whether or not the relationship constituted anything more than a *sense* of spiritual communion on the part of the poet is a needless question. It was the figure who counted, not as flesh and blood but as abstract object of the need of this poet. Thomas Higginson, at this particular time and, for the poet's particular needs, could serve this sustaining function.

24. The two letters of 1863 (L–280 and L–282) and the single letter of 1864 (L–290) have no information pertinent to this study. Higginson had taken command of a Union Army regiment in November 1862 and consequently was too occupied in this period to encourage the poet to continue an active correspondence.

25. Higginson, "Letter to a Young Contributor," p. 403.

26. *Ibid.*, *passim*.

27. Josiah Gilbert Holland (1819–1881) founded *Scribner's Monthly* in 1870 and was its editor until his death. He and his wife, Elizabeth Chapin Holland (1823–1896) were close friends of Emily Dickinson.

28. The supposition that the "Two Editors" were Bowles and Holland is also offered by Johnson in *An Interpretive Biography*, p. 112.

29. Higginson, "Letter to a Young Contributor," p. 407.

30. *Ibid.*, p. 401.

31. *Letters*, II, 403.

32. Compare the attitude in this poem to "I meant to have but modest needs — " (P-476). The last stanza reads in part:

> . . . I, grown shrewder — scan the Skies
> With a suspicious Air —
> As Children — swindled for the first
> All Swindlers — be — infer —

CHAPTER II: Aspiration and Its Analogues

1. Whicher, *This Was a Poet*, p. 288.
2. Jay Leyda, *The Years and Hours of Emily Dickinson*, 2 vols. (New Haven, 1960), I, xix.
3. Louis Untermeyer, *Modern American Poetry Mid-Century Edition* (New York, 1950), p. 7.
4. *Ibid.*, p. 9.
5. R. P. Blackmur, "Emily Dickinson: Notes on Prejudice and Fact," *The Expense of Greatness* (New York, 1940), p. 138.
6. Yvor Winters, *In Defense of Reason* (Denver, 1947), p. 284.
7. Leyda, *The Years and Hours of Emily Dickinson*, I, xxi.
8. Chase, *Emily Dickinson*, p. 121.
9. *Ibid.*, p. 142.
10. Johnson, *An Interpretive Biography*, p. 151.
11. Anderson, *Stairway of Surprise*, p. xiii. The plan of Anderson's study makes a more general classification of the poems into those concerned with the "outer" world, the "inner" world, and the "other" world.
12. Leyda, *The Years and Hours of Emily Dickinson*, I, xx.
13. *The Letters of John Keats 1814–1821*, ed. H. E. Rollins, 2 vols. (Cambridge, Mass., 1958), I, 224.
14. See the fine discussion of the cultural phenomena of the "sisterhood of sensibility" and the "Eden of eternal adolescence" in W. R. Taylor and Christopher Lasch, "Two 'Kindred Spirits': Sorority and Family in New England, 1839–1846," *New England Quarterly*, March 1963.
15. Samuel Bowles, editor of the *Springfield Daily Republican*, was the recipient of this poem. *Poems*, I, 36.
16. Among the early poems the following are concerned specifically with the moment of death: numbers 27, 45, 71, 75, 144, 146, 149, 150, 158, 241, 255, and 287.
17. Thomas Mann, *The Magic Mountain*, trans. H. T. Lowe-Porter (New York, 1955), pp. 26–27.
18. The early poems in which representation of the spectacle of nature is the central purpose include numbers 6, 11, 12, 15, 17, 19, 36,

41, 64, 74, 81, 99, 110, 111, 116, 120, 133, 138, 140, 142, 152, 157, 173, 198, 204, 214, and 219.

19. The ritualistic quality of nature is described also in poems 18, 22, 100, and 155.

20. R. P. Blackmur, "Emily Dickinson's Notation," *Kenyon Review*, 18:230 (1956).

21. Santayana declared a similar concern to be the basic thematic material in the work of Goethe: "Goethe never depicts . . . the object his hero is pursuing; he is satisfied with depicting the pursuit." *Three Philosophical Poets: Lucretius, Dante, and Goethe* (Cambridge, Mass., 1922), p. 142.

22. Richard Wilbur, "Sumptuous Destitution," *Emily Dickinson: Three Views* (Amherst, Mass., 1960), p. 36.

23. Gay Wilson Allen, *American Prosody* (American Book Company, 1935), p. 319.

24. Cf. Michael Polanyi, *Personal Knowledge: Towards a Post-Critical Philosophy* (Chicago, 1960), p. 200.

25. Ernst Gombrich, *Meditations on a Hobby Horse and Other Essays on the Theory of Art* (Greenwich, Conn., 1964), p. 18.

26. *The Letters of John Keats 1814–1821*, I, 185.

27. Johann Goethe, *Faust*, pt. 1, trans. Philip Wayne (Baltimore, 1961), p. 82.

28. *Letters*, III, 922. Emily Dickinson seems to have continued in a tendency of the New England mind which, according to Perry Miller, had its beginnings in Jonathan Edwards and extended through the work and thought of Emerson. He writes: "From the time of Edwards to that of Emerson, the husks of puritanism were being discarded, but the energies of many puritans were not yet diverted — they could not be diverted — from a passionate search of the soul and of nature, from the quest to which Calvinism had devoted them" ("Jonathan Edwards to Emerson," *New England Quarterly*, 13:617 [December 1940]). See also Albert J. Gelpi, *Emily Dickinson — The Mind of the Poet* (Cambridge, Mass., 1965), especially chap. iv, "Seeing New Englandly: From Edwards to Emerson to Dickinson," for an excellent elaboration of Miller's view and a confirmation of mine.

CHAPTER III: The Quester and the Queen

1. Archibald MacLeish, *Emily Dickinson: Three Views* (Amherst, Mass., 1960), pp. 19–21. Cf. Gelpi, *Emily Dickinson — The Mind of the Poet*, pp. 126–127.

2. See Ernst Gombrich's discussion of the artist-object relationship in *Art and Illusion: A Study in the Psychology of Pictorial Representation*, 2nd ed. (New York, 1961), p. 90.

3. The circus figure is so unusual one may speculate that it was suggested by Emerson's poem "Threnody." Near the close of that poem Emerson asserts the hospitable atmosphere of the heaven God had made:

> Not of adamant and gold
> Built he heaven stark and cold;
> No, but a nest of bending reeds,
> Flowering grass, and scented weeds;
> Or like a traveller's fleeing tent,
> Or bow above the tempest bent;
> Built of tears and sacred flames,
> And virtue reaching to its aims;
> Built of furtherance and pursuing
> Not of spent deeds, but of doing.

4. *Letters*, III, 924.

5. John Crowe Ransom, "Emily Dickinson," *Perspectives USA*, no. 15 (Spring 1956), p. 20.

CHAPTER IV: Devotional Form and the Constant Occasion for Irony

1. George Saintsbury, *Historical Manual of English Prosody* (London, 1930), p. 281.

2. *Ibid.*, p. 272.

3. Emily Dickinson employed particular elements characteristic of the ballad, however. Anderson's summary of this point is useful: "Though rarely adopting the ballad's narrative structure, she took advantage of some of its qualities: the strong colloquial idioms, the roughened meters and proximate rhymes, and especially the swift climactic movement that overleaped sequences in its passion for conciseness." *Stairway of Surprise*, p. 25.

4. The quotation is from *Isaac Watts Hymns and Spiritual Songs 1707–1748: A Study in Early Eighteenth Century Language Changes*, ed. Selma L. Bishop (London, 1962), p. li.

5. Winters, *In Defense of Reason*, p. 296.

6. Saintsbury, *Historical Manual of English Prosody*, p. 290.

7. Each hymn in *Watts's Church Psalmody: A Collection of Psalms and Hymns, Adapted to Public Worship* (Boston, 1854), a copy of which was in the Dickinson family library, is labeled as to its metrical arrangement. A concise description of the various forms is in Johnson, *An Interpretive Biography*, pp. 85–86.

8. Johnson, *An Interpretive Biography*, p. 85. Poems dated earlier than 1861 which are most irregular are the following: in general iambic movements, numbers 5, 10, 33, 34, 38, 47, 60, 63, 73, 84, 92, 120, 135, 136, 155, 156, 160, 162, 177, 192, 199, 200, 209, and 216; in mark-

edly mixed movement, numbers 11, 21, 22, 29, 35, 37, 40, 43, 49, 51, 52, 57, 66, 68, 69, 85, 86, 95, 102, 110, 113, 139, 141, 153, 158, 182, 187, 190, 193, and 196.

9. *Ibid.*, p. 85. A copy of *Watts's Church Psalmody* in Amherst College Library has the name of Emily Dickinson's father embossed on the front and back covers.

10. *The Psalms of David Imitated in the Language of the New Testament, and Adapted to the Christian Use and Worship. By I. Watts, D.D. . . . To the Psalms is Added, A Selection of Hymns*, ed. Timothy Dwight (Hartford, 1830), no page number.

11. Henry W. Foote, *Three Centuries of American Hymnody* (Cambridge, Mass., 1940), pp. 187-188.

12. Millicent T. Bingham, *Emily Dickinson's Home* (New York, 1955), pp. 35-36.

For a discussion of Watts's influence on Emily Dickinson, see James Davidson, "Emily Dickinson and Isaac Watts," *Boston Public Library Quarterly*, 6:141-149 (July 1954). In addition to arguing persuasively that Watts is the source of the verse forms, Mr. Davidson makes the significant distinction that whereas Watts saw man as depraved, Emily Dickinson was in revolt against this Calvinist dogma. The point, though perhaps stated too strongly, suggests the embodied irony in Emily Dickinson's use of the hymn as vehicle for some irreligious thoughts and emotions.

13. Noted by Johnson in *Poems*, I, 83. The quotations of Watts are from *The Psalms, Hymns, and Spiritual Songs*, ed. Samuel Worcester (Boston, 1827). This hymn is number 66, pp. 413-414.

14. Poems of regular metrical pattern or with only slight variation are numbers 1, 3, 7, 9, 12, 13, 15, 16, 18, 19, 20, 23, 24, 25, 26, 30, 31, 32, 36, 41, 53, 55, 58, 59, 61, 62, 64, 67, 70, 71, 75, 77, 79, 81, 82, 83, 87, 88, 89, 90, 91, 93, 97, 98, 99, 100, 103, 104, 106, 107, 111, 112, 115, 117, 118, 121, 122, 124, 125, 126, 128, 129, 130, 131, 132, 133, 140, 145, 147, 149, 150, 154, 157, 159, 161, 164, 172, 174, 179, 181, 183, 185, 186, 188, 189, 194, 195, 198, 201, 202, 206, 207, 208, 210, 214, 217, 219, 220, 222, 223, 224, 229, 233, 235, 237, 239, 242, 243, 246, 247, 254, 255, 259, 262, 264, 265, 268, 270, 271, 272, 273, 275, 277, 280, 282, 286, 287, 290, 293, 294, 330, and 687. Poems of iambic movement but with mixed syllabic patterns are numbers 2, 8, 14, 17, 42, 44, 45, 46, 48, 50, 54, 56, 74, 78, 80, 105, 116, 134, 142, 143, 144, 146, 148, 152, 165, 166, 167, 169, 171, 173, 178, 180, 184, 191, 204, 205, 232, 234, 241, 256, 263, 274, and 278. Poems of iambic movement but with little regularity of pattern are numbers 5, 10, 33, 34, 38, 47, 60, 63, 73, 84, 92, 96, 120, 135, 136, 155, 156, 160, 162, 177, 192, 199, 200, 209, 216, 218, 225, 226, 236, 244, 245, 252, 253, 257, 258, 260, 261, 279, 281, 283, 284, 285, 288, 289, 296, 297, and 298.

15. This is the verse form most persistent in Emily Dickinson's poetry. In the early years common meter is used in unvaried pattern in fifty-nine poems; in thirty-seven others it forms the metrical base. These ninety-six poems account for almost a third of the poetry in the formative period. Other forms appear considerably less often. Regular "sevens and sixes," for example, structures only twenty-six. Of iambic verse in *irregular* metrical pattern, there are in these years forty-seven poems, the most persistent use of this free form occurring in the work of 1861 (see n. 14 above).

Poems in regular common meter are numbers 26, 30, 31, 62, 70, 75, 77, 79, 81, 82, 83, 99, 107, 111, 112, 115, 117, 124, 131, 133, 149, 154, 161, 164, 181, 183, 189, 194, 198, 201, 202, 208, 210, 214, 217, 219, 220, 221, 222, 223, 224, 237, 239, 242, 243, 246, 254, 255, 262, 264, 271, 272, 273, 280, 282, 286, 290, 293, and 330. Poems with a discernible common meter base are 8, 14, 17, 42, 44, 45, 46, 48, 50, 54, 56, 74, 78, 80, 105, 116, 134, 142, 144, 146, 148, 152, 165, 167, 169, 171, 173, 178, 180, 184, 191, 232, 234, 241, 256, 274, 278.

16. Anderson suggests the doctrinal aspect of Emily Dickinson's use of the hymn form: "though she transmutes [the standard form of devotional music] from the ritual hymn in celebration of an accepted creed, it is always there in the background of the reader's consciousness as a point from which to measure the spiritual adventure of a schismatic soul." *Stairway of Surprise*, p. 25.

17. R. P. Blackmur, "Religious Poetry in America," *University — A Princeton Magazine*, 9:18 (Summer 1961).

CHAPTER V: Motion, Rest, and Metamorphosis

1. Chase, *Emily Dickinson*, p. 223.
2. Whicher, *This Was a Poet*, p. 264.
3. "Introduction," Jonathan Edwards, *Images or Shadows of Divine Things*, ed. Perry Miller (New Haven, 1948), p. 4.
4. *Ibid.*, p. 11.
5. Blackmur, *The Expense of Greatness*, pp. 134–135.
6. Archibald MacLeish, *Poetry and Experience* (Cambridge, Mass., 1961), p. 96.
7. Whicher, *This Was a Poet*, p. 288.
8. *Letters*, I, 150–151.
9. Miller, ed., *Images or Shadows of Divine Things*, pp. 4–5.
10. Blackmur, *The Expense of Greatness*, p. 136.
11. In a letter dated 1873 (L–386) a significant change in attitude is apparent. Here the poet declares that the sea-like existence is not made more comforting by the knowledge that harbors may exist. To her recipient, she writes: "I hope that you have Power and as much of Peace

as in our deep existence may be possible. To multiply the Harbors does not reduce the Sea." *Letters*, II, 503.

CHAPTER VI: Audible Correlatives of Emotional Tension

1. Whicher, *This Was a Poet*, p. 248.
2. "Emily Dickinson's Letters," *Atlantic Monthly*, 68:446 (October 1891).
3. Allen, *American Prosody*, p. 319.
4. Edward Sapir suggests that though Emily Dickinson's rhymes are awkward, they influenced practices in twentieth-century poetry: "So ardent was her spirit that an almost comic gaucherie in the finding of rhymes could not prevent her from discovering to us the promise of a fresh, primitive, and relentless school of poetry that is still on the way." "Emily Dickinson, A Primitive," *Poetry*, 26:99 (May 1925). F. L. Pattee dismissed her approximate rhymes as evidence of serious weakness: "To every normal ear these are discords, positive defects that not even genius can surmount." "Gentian, Not Rose: The Real Emily Dickinson," *Sewanee Review*, 54:194 (April–June 1937).
5. Gombrich, *Art and Illusion*, p. 90.
6. René Wellek and Austin Warren, *Theory of Literature* (New York, 1949), p. 161.
7. D. S. R. Welland, *Wilfred Owen: A Critical Study* (London, 1960), p. 105.
8. *Ibid.*, pp. 108–109.
9. Johnson, *An Interpretive Biography*, p. 87.
10. Poem numbers 1, 2, 3, 4, 5, 6, 7, 10, 11, 12, 13, 15, 17, 19, 22, 23, 24, 25, 26, 27, 28, 29, 30, 31, 32, 33, 34, 36, 37, 38, 41, 43, 44, 46, 47, 48, 49, 50, 52, 53, 56, 57, 58, 60, 61, 62, 66, 67, 69, 71, 72, 74, 75, 76, 78, 82, 85, 87, 88, 89, 92, 93, 95, 101, 102, 103, 104, 105, 106, 107, 108, 109, 110, 111, 113, 114, 117, 119, 121, 122, 123, 124, 126, 127, 128, 129, 130, 131, 132, 136, 138, 140, 142, 143, 144, 146, 147, 149, 150, 151, 152, 154, 155, 156, 157, 158, 161, 162, 163, 164, 167, 168, 170, 171, 173, 174, 178, 179, 181, 182, 183, 184, 185, 186, 189, 191, 193, 195, 196, 198, 201, 204, 206, 207, 211, 212, 213, 217, 218, 221, 226, 227, 228, 230, 231, 232, 233, 235, 236, 239, 240, 245, 249, 250, 251, 253, 256, 257, 258, 259, 265, 267, 268, 271, 274, 277, 278, 282, 284, 285, 287, 288, 289, 292, 297, 298, 331, and 687.
11. The frequency of these various types of rhyme in Emily Dickinson's early poetry is in a slightly different order: exact rhymes, as indicated in the text, account for about one in two occasions; suspended, about one in four; vowel, about one in twelve; identical and imperfect, about one in thirty; and eye, about one in one hundred.
12. Jules Romains termed this kind of device *accord renversé*. One of

his examples is *riche-chère*, quoted in Welland, *Wilfred Owen: A Critical Study*, p. 109.

13. Anderson, *Stairway of Surprise*, p. 27.

14. Saintsbury, *Historical Manual of English Prosody*, p. 17.

15. Johnson, *An Interpretive Biography*, p. 97.

16. *Ibid.*, p. 87.

17. Welland similarly shows the artistic propriety of Wilfred Owen's approximate rhyming to his view of himself and the world. Owens' experiments in half-rhyme, Welland writes, "reflected better than rhyme the disintegration of values in the world . . . It [also] offered a unique and perfect expression to that diffidence and lack of self-confidence that all who knew him record, and at the same time it coincided with the hesitant sense of frustration that his poetry had to communicate." *Wilfred Owen: A Critical Study*, p. 119.

18. *Letters*, II, 408.

19. *Letters*, III, 661.

20. *Letters*, II, 644.

CHAPTER VII: New Ways of Articulating the World

1. Chase, *Emily Dickinson*, p. 226.

2. Wylie Sypher, *Rococo to Cubism in Art and Literature* (New York, 1960), p. 43.

3. Chase, *Emily Dickinson*, p. 221.

4. Henry Wells, *Introduction to Emily Dickinson* (Chicago, 1947), p. 285.

5. R. P. Blackmur, *Language as Gesture* (New York, 1952), p. 44.

6. William Howard, "Emily Dickinson's Poetic Vocabulary," *PMLA*, 72:225–248 (1957). This is a comprehensive study of the poet's vocabulary, and though its conclusions are based largely on statistical findings, and are therefore of limited value in reading particular poems, the study corrects the persistent belief in the poet's eccentricity, rigidity, and subjectivity, and places her squarely in the English tradition.

7. Chase, *Emily Dickinson*, p. 145.

8. Howard, "Emily Dickinson's Poetic Vocabulary," p. 247.

9. *Ibid.*, p. 243. The seventeen words (with the number of appearances in parentheses) arranged by part of speech — adjectives, nouns, verbs — are: little (226), day (268), life (194), eye (177), sun (175), man (175), face (157), time (155), bird (153), heaven (153), know (354), go (276), come (227), see (219), make (175), tell (168), die (153).

10. *Ibid.*, p. 248.

11. See Stuart Robertson, *The Development of Modern English* (Englewood Cliffs, N. J., 1961), p. 285: "It is true that the inflected sub-

junctive (or optative) of Old English is now a remnant, and that the meaning it used to express — of possibility, hypothesis, wish, and so on — are [sic] now expressed also by such function-words as *can, may, ought*."

12. Chase, *Emily Dickinson*, p. 106.

13. Whicher, *This Was a Poet*, p. 234.

14. Johnson, *An Interpretive Biography*, p. 93.

15. Anderson uses a variant text, not the packet copy but the version sent to Susan Gilbert Dickinson. Cf. *Poems*, II, 522–523.

16. Anderson, *Stairway of Surprise*, p. 67.

17. Higginson, "Emily Dickinson's Letters," p. 444.

18. Ransom, "Emily Dickinson," p. 7.

19. Other representative early poems in which capitalization seems to have a similar intent are numbers 233, 234, 235, 241, 263, and 264.

20. Susanne Langer sees this phenomenon as the unique communicative value of poetry: "To understand the 'idea' in a work of art is . . . more like *having a new experience than like entertaining a new proposition*." *Philosophy in a New Key: A Study in the Symbolism of Reason, Rite, and Art* (Cambridge, Mass., 1942), p. 263.

21. Samuel Worcester, "Extracts from the Editor's Preface," in Watts's *Psalms* . . . , pp. vi–vii.

22. "Nature is a Haunted House — but Art — a House that tries to be haunted" (L–459a). *Letters*, II, 554.

23. Johnson says: "Quite properly such 'punctuation' can be omitted in later editions." *Poems*, I, lxiii. I believe he has since modified this view.

24. G. F. Whicher declares this "playing with words" is a mannerism Emily Dickinson acquired from the native humor of her time. *This Was a Poet*, p. 205.

25. Chase, *Emily Dickinson*, p. 236.

CHAPTER VIII: The Early Achievement

1. Charles Anderson judges that her "really fine poems" number about one hundred and that about twenty-five constitute the body of her "great ones" (*Stairway of Surprise*, pp. xiii–xiv). In his group of superior works he includes no fewer than ten poems from the formative period, and he asserts that the two additional early poems "Safe in their Alabaster Chambers" (P–216) and "A Clock stopped" (P–287) definitely belong to the small group of highest achievement (*ibid., passim*). The ten early poems referred to in Anderson's discussions of the "really fine" works are "One dignity delays for all" (P–98), "What Inn is this" (P–115), "These are the days when Birds come back" (P–130), "How many times these low feet staggered" (P–187), "I taste a liquor never brewed" (P–214), "Blazing in Gold and quenching in Purple" (P–228),

"Wild Nights — Wild Nights!" (P-249), "There's a certain Slant of light" (P-258), "I felt a Funeral, in my Brain" (P-280), and "Of Bronze — and Blaze" (P-290). Richard Chase's study also confirms her early achievement. Among what he terms the "dozen or two [poems which] urge one to use the word 'great,'" he includes the five early poems "How many times these low feet staggered" (P-187), "Safe in their Alabaster Chambers" (P-216), "There's a certain Slant of Light" (P-258), "The only Ghost I ever saw" (P-274), and "I felt a Funeral, in my Brain" (P-280) (*Emily Dickinson*, pp. 119, 170, 173, 198, 203, 233, 247). In combination, Chase's and Anderson's conclusions provide a minimal list of at least six early works to be regarded as first-rate.

2. See the Index of First Lines for complete cross references to the texts of the poems and to my discussions of them.

3. Mark Van Doren declares of her work in general: "No greater mistake could be made than to suppose that her triumphs of language were unpremeditated." *Letters of Emily Dickinson*, ed. Mabel L. Todd (Cleveland, 1951), p. xiii.

INDEX OF FIRST LINES

Italic numerals indicate pages on which full or partial citations from the poems appear.

GENERAL INDEX

Allen, Gay Wilson, 38, 106–107
Anderson, Charles R., 1–2, 19, 116–117, 138, 191n, 193n, 196n
Atlantic Monthly, 3–10

Blackmur, R. P., 17, 33, 73–74, 88, 99, 104, 134
Bowles, Samuel, 9
Bowles, Mrs. Samuel, 45
Browning, Robert, 120
Bryant, William Cullen, 81

Chase, Richard, ix, 18, 19, 78–79, 125–126, 135, 137–138, 153, 197n
Crane, Stephen, xii

Dickinson, [William] Austin, 23, 59, 90–92
Dickinson, Edward, 46, 58
Dickinson, Emily: correspondence with Higginson, 1–15, 41, 122–123, 175; desire to publish, 9, 15; early assurance, 7–15, 156, 175; early canon, xi–xii; early poetic development, ix, xi, 1–15, 156, 174; early pose of artlessness, 1–7; her creative mind, 156, 190n28; oblique vision, 121–124; tragic understanding, 156; varying attitudes, 37–38, 40–54, 74, 89, 105, 157, 174. The poetry: concision, x, 20, 38–39, 68, 73, 135, 154–155, 157–163, 175; control, ix, 54, 73, 157, 175; controlling theme, 16–39, 156–157, 174; dissociated emotion, 50, 72, 88, 175; hymn meters, 55–74, 115–117, 157, 171, 175; imagery, 23–24, 62, 75–104, 149–150; private typology, 76, 81–83, 91; problem of chronology, xi–xii; rhyme variations, 106–124, 157, 165, 175, 194n4, 194n11; senti-

mental cult, 24, 38; speaker in the poems, 40–54; illusion of spontaneity, ix, 48, 120, 143, 157; structural patterns, 118–121, 131–134; vocabulary, 134–136. Stylistic mannerisms, x, 125–155, 157; capitalization, 140–142; dash, 142–145; disregard of convention, 9–10, 15, 55, 70–72; personification, 28, 152–153; "rococo" manner, 125–129; shifting symbolic values, 97–104, 153; style in letters, 8, 15; "subjunctive," 136–139; word tricks, 145–152
Dickinson, Emily Norcross, 45
Dickinson, Lavinia, 45
Donne, John, 21, 120
Dwight, Timothy, 58

Edwards, Jonathan, 81–82, 91, 190n
Emerson, Ralph Waldo, 171, 190n, 191n
Enceladus, 23, 33
Everyman, 104

Faust, 39
Foote, Henry W., 58–59
Frost, Robert, 21
Frye, Northrup, 3

Goethe, Johann, 39, 190n
Gombrich, Ernst, x, xii, 39, 107

Herbert, George, 104
Higginson, Thomas Wentworth, xi, xii, 1, 3–15, 19, 41, 106, 122–123, 140, 175; "Letter to a Young Contributor," 3–6, 9–10
Holland, Josiah Gilbert, 7–8, 9
Holland, Mrs. Josiah Gilbert, 7–8
Hopkins, Gerard Manley, 108
Howard, William, 134–136